Although Billy Roberts has been psych̶ he left school in 1962 at the age of 16 he was already living the dream of every other teenage boy – playing lead guitar in a rock band, touring Europe with some of the biggest names in the world of music: The Yardbirds, The Moody Blues, The Small Faces. The highlight of his career was having a meal with Jimi Hendrix in Paris. Billy went on to be one of the UK's top stage psychics, and is today regarded as a leading authority on metaphysical and esoteric sciences. In 1983 he founded The Thought Workshop, one of the UK's first centres for psychic and spiritual studies and alternative therapies. He has appeared on television all over the world, and in 2003 was commissioned by Sony to appear in a documentary to promote their Playstation 2 Game *Ghost Hunter*, filmed on location in New Orleans. He has also made several appearances on the popular television programme *Most Haunted*, and has presented his own Channel One Television series, *Secrets of the Paranormal*. Today he continues to conduct workshops and seminars in many countries, specializing in the process of psychic development and self-improvement.

www.billyroberts.co.uk

By the same author

So You Want to be Psychic?

Billy Roberts

WATKINS PUBLISHING
LONDON

This edition first published in the UK and USA 2010 by
Watkins Publishing, Sixth Floor, Castle House,
75–76 Wells Street, London W1T 3QH

1 3 5 7 9 10 8 6 4 2

Designed by Jerry Goldie
Printed and bound by Imago in China

British Library Cataloguing-in-Publication Data Available

Library of Congress Cataloging-in-Publication Data Available

ISBN: 978-1-906787-96-7

www.watkinspublishing.co.uk

Distributed in the USA and Canada by Sterling Publishing Co., Inc.
387 Park Avenue South, New York, NY 10016-8810

For information about custom editions, special sales, premium and
corporate purchases, please contact Sterling Special Sales
Department at 800-805-5489 or specialsales@sterlingpub.com

Contents

To my wife Dolly
for her love and support

Introduction

s with the majority of mediums, my earliest recollections of psychic experience go back to when I was three years old. As a result of a serious respiratory disease I spent most of my early life either in hospital, or in bed at home. As a direct consequence I was a very introverted child and, being denied the company of other children, was forced to spend most of my time alone. Looking back it is now clear that this affected me both emotionally and psychologically. Little wonder then that I felt quite different to other children. I was so accustomed to my ghostly visitors that they appeared as real to me as everyone else. One could say that seeing so-called 'dead' people was commonplace to me, and it was only by the age of nine that I realized that other children were not the same as me.

Because of my teacher's growing concern for my psychological health, it was suggested that I should see a child psychologist. During my two-hour consultation with the psychologist I was shown abstract pictures, coloured shapes, and asked a series of nonsensical questions that sent my young mind into a near state of utter confusion. The young doctor's diagnosis was that, as a consequence of my serious health condition, I was highly sensitive, insecure, and creative with an overactive imagination. She was correct of course. However, her prognosis that I would probably grow out of it was very wrong – I did not! This was the mid-1950s when attitudes towards such abilities had changed very little from Victorian times, when anyone with paranormal skills would be sectioned and placed in an asylum.

However, today, thank God, things have changed a lot. These days there is a greater understanding of the paranormal and the psychic abilities of children. In fact, today, as a result of the way mediums and the paranormal are portrayed on television, a whole new psychology concerning psychic abilities has evolved. More and more people are becoming increasingly aware of their own psychic potential, and are seeking guidance and ways to cultivate this even further. In response to the great need for education where psychic abilities are concerned, in 1983 I founded The Thought Workshop, the northwest's first centre for psychic and spiritual studies and alternative therapies. Here some of the UK's most knowledgeable teachers held courses, workshops and seminars, attended by students from all over the world.

Although The Thought Workshop was dissolved in 1990, I still take my workshops and seminars all over the world, and am frequently invited to hold talks and give lectures in colleges and centres in the UK and abroad. *So You Want to be Psychic?* is a handbook based on over 30 years of teaching experiences which have helped hundreds of students of psychic science to become working mediums, psychics and healers. I am sure what I have put together will help you to safely develop your psychic abilities and reach your full psychic potential.

In these liberated times we no longer feel the need to glance cautiously over our shoulder before whispering the old taboo words such as 'paranormal', 'psychic' or 'supernatural'. Today these words raise few eyebrows – quite the contrary in fact, as a quick check through any weekly television listings will show. You will doubtless spot more than a couple of programmes concerned, in one way or another, with psychic and supernatural matters. A certain sort of, dare I say, 'credibility' seems currently to be hovering around the edges of the paranormal.

So, just what are our psychic abilities, and why should we strive to develop them? What, if anything, is in it for us?

These psychic powers about which we hear so much these days

are, broadly speaking, those abilities for which contemporary science has no explanation. Clairvoyance, healing, precognition, telepathy and mediumship are all examples of psychic abilities. By developing your psychic powers you will gain much greater control of your own life. You will find yourself becoming more assertive and positive in both outlook and approach. Your psychic *self* will help you to achieve your aims and reach your goals.

Before we evolved even the most rudimentary form of speech, it is believed that our prehistoric forebears communicated their thoughts and feelings telepathically. Maurice Maeterlinck once said, 'We only developed speech so that we could lie.'

Whether or not the latter indictment is true, telepathy is the underlying principle of mediumship and various other psychic phenomena. Of one thing we can rest assured, that modern man has most certainly forgotten, if not lost completely, most of the psychic abilities possessed by his primitive ancestors. The reason for this loss is simple. Modern man, living as he does today, would have little use for his ancestors' psychic skills. How would they fit into this age of science, technology and 'reason'?

Psychic development today is, therefore, not so much a case of receiving knowledge as it is of *remembering*. With this in mind, it is not my intention in this book to teach you anything, I will merely try to remind you of what you have long since forgotten.

From my own experience, I know only too well just how difficult it is to choose something suitable from the innumerable books displayed in bookshops today. So many of them offer a variety of quick and easy methods for developing your own psychic abilities; how do you pick the one that is right for you? This can often dishearten the most sincere 'student' of psychic develop- ment who, finding it all too confusing, may therefore decide not to pursue the subject further.

Having myself encountered many of the problems and pitfalls

which pave the road of the whole process of psychic development, I have put together a few ideas and designed a series of programmes which I feel may be of some help to you as you move towards the development and expansion of your *psychic self*. My approach to psychic development is purely holistic, with the sole intention of cultivating all the senses as opposed to one. In the long run you will find this more beneficial and far more effective.

Remember the ancient precept: 'When the student is ready the teacher will always appear.' This is as right and meaningful today as it was when it was first written. For, in my experience, when the time is right the opportunity will always present itself. This opportunity may be anything from a chance meeting with a knowledgeable teacher, to a book whose title almost jumps out at you from its place on a shelf in your local bookstore.

However, there are no short routes where psychic development is concerned; no corners that can be cut. Your endeavour to develop your psychic faculties may, in fact, be an extremely difficult and at times painful task, during which you need to be keenly vigilant, extremely patient and certainly self-critical.

Always beware of praise and flattery, for whether or not it is honestly given, it can lull you into a false sense of security, causing complacency and vanity, both of which are extremely self-destructive where the science of psychic development is concerned.

I have found the process of psychic development to be an extremely solitary and even lonely path to follow. Its call for total dedication can disrupt one's social life. On the other hand, it does have its rewards, not least of which is the development of a fuller and more complete awareness of the world in which one lives, and a greater realization of the soul and its independence of the physical body.

I have never believed that it is enough to merely develop the psychic faculties by themselves, so to speak, while having little or no knowledge of their background and mechanics, i.e. of what they are, how and why they work and where they come from. One would not expect a surgeon to perform delicate and complicated operations without any prior knowledge of the physiological and anatomical components that make up the man.

I am frequently reminded of the profound words of the 19th-century mystic and dramatist Maurice Maeterlinck.

The wise man is not he who sees, but he who seeing furthest, has the greatest love and understanding for all mankind. He who sees without loving and understanding is only straining his eyes in the darkness.

Maeterlinck's words speak volumes, I feel. It is with this sentiment in mind that I have included in Chapter One a description of man's subtle anatomy, the aura, and the mechanics of the process of psychic development. Over the years I have made a detailed study of various methods and techniques of meditation, and of exercises for quietening the mind. From these I have created a programme of meditation that is extremely effective in the precipitation of psychic awareness, which is also included in the text. Readers should first read the book through, and then select that which is appropriate and which will work most effectively for them. One of the main obstacles one faces when endeavouring to develop one's psychic abilities is the doubt that it can ever be successfully achieved. Thus it is important to realize that everyone possesses psychic powers potentially, and it is wrong to surmise that a psychic ability that is not immediately apparent cannot be developed and cultivated.

Of course, some people do have greater potential than others, and may, therefore, develop their skills in a shorter period of time. Nonetheless, the potential to develop psychic powers lies within each and every one of us, and can most certainly be encouraged and developed with the use of specific techniques.

It is also wrong to assume that a psychic ability which one already possesses cannot in any way be refined and developed further. A psychic power is like any other mental ability – it most certainly can be improved upon and developed to its fullest potential.

I do have to say, however, that I'm not advocating that everyone should set about developing their psychic abilities. On the contrary, the whole process of psychic development may have an adverse effect on the psychological nature of some people, and it is therefore vitally important that, before endeavouring to cultivate the psychic faculties, appropriate emotional, psychological and spiritual preparation should take place.

How Psychic Are You?

- Do you ever sense that the telephone is going to ring, and it does?

- Do you sometimes know what your partner is going to say just before they speak?

- Do you ever have strong feelings about something that is going to happen, and it does?

- Have you ever been alone in the house and suddenly felt as though someone is watching you, or standing behind you?

- Have you ever felt uncomfortable while sitting alone in a theatre or waiting in a bus queue, and when you looked over your shoulder someone was staring at you?

- Do you ever dream of specific things or situations that later happen?

- Do you ever see pinpoints of intense bright light around people's heads, or pinpoints of colour floating in the air?

- Have you ever seen a coloured mist around people or animals?
- Have you ever thought you have seen a shadowy figure out of the corner of your eye while you were alone in the house?
- Have you ever met someone for the first time and felt certain that you know them from somewhere, although you don't?
- Have you ever walked into a house for the first time and immediately been overwhelmed by its warmth; coldness; happiness; sadness?
- When you are drifting into sleep do you ever hear someone calling your name?
- Have you ever been overwhelmed by a fragrance that no one else can smell, and which reminds you of a dead relative or friend?
- Have you ever handled a piece of antique jewellery and found pictures and impressions forming in your mind?
- Have strong feelings ever forewarned you not to go to a certain place or do a particular thing?
- Have you ever had bad feelings about someone whom everyone else likes?
- When someone is unwell do you ever feel compelled to place your hands on them in an attempt to make them better?
- Have you ever seen patterns on curtains or carpets change into faces?
- Have you ever been overwhelmed with the feeling that a relative or friend, living on the other side of the world, has had an accident, and you later learned that they had?
- Have you ever felt compelled to write a poem or piece of philosophical writing which, on later examination, appears completely alien to the way you think?

It is quite common to have experienced two or perhaps three of the things listed above. However, to have experienced six or seven of them does show that you have psychic potential. If you answer 'yes' to ten, or even all the things listed, you most certainly do have a higher than average psychic potential. Read on.

Chapter One

The Aura

If you want to be trendy and New Age these days, all you have to do is talk about the aura with some authority. Unfortunately, the aura's newfound popularity has led it to become a greatly misunderstood aspect of man's subtle anatomy. Obviously, the word 'aura' is often used without any understanding of its true meaning. We have all heard, for example, the expressions 'He has an aura of serenity about him', or 'The house has an aura of happiness and warmth'. However, the word 'aura' is far more than a descriptive term; today it is both a metaphysical phenomenon and a scientific fact. In fact, the word aura suggests the existence of a subtle atmosphere emanating from, and surrounding, all living things.

What is the Aura?

I suppose the aura is best and most simply described as a vaporous mass of electromagnetic particles surrounding both animate and inanimate matter. It is, in fact, an incredible energy field of varying degrees of vibration. However, the aura that emanates from the human form differs greatly from that which emanates from an inanimate object, inasmuch as the human aura represents the degree of life and consciousness present. Although the presence of life in both animate and inanimate matter is measured in degrees, the aura that emanates from animate matter is completely different in both appearance and movement from that which emanates from inanimate matter, even though life is still present in inanimate objects, albeit at a lower level.

In comparison to the aura of an inanimate object (such as a chair or table), the human aura is a veritable kaleidoscope of colours, and is full of movement as it radiates outward from the body. In the human aura the degree or level of vitality present in the body is exhibited in the consistency of outpouring energy, and the health of the person to whom the aura belongs is thus represented by the varying combinations and frequency of colours, their shades and intensities.

The human aura is, in fact, more luminous than the inanimate aura, and changes with the person's passing thoughts, feelings and emotional impulses. Therefore, the one who is able to perceive the human energy field in its totality (and not just one or two aspects of it) is able to gain access to an abundance of personal information about the person to whom the aura belongs. The individual who possesses the ability to actually 'see' the aura (and this is, of course, a psychic skill) is able to determine a person's mental, emotional and physical health. The spiritual progress which a person has attained is also apparent in the aura along with other significant corresponding data. It therefore makes sense that as long as what is seen in the aura is interpreted correctly, a person's true character should be revealed. And I do mean the *true* character because, to the one who possesses the ability to 'see' the aura, the truth will always be clearly visible behind the mask of falsehood. The aura is, in fact, a database containing everything about the individual's nature.

The aura has been discussed and depicted in many ways over thousands of years in religious, cultural and artistic circles. An obvious example is the headdress of a Native American chief, which traditionally symbolizes the aura and its many colours. The beautiful display of colour in the headdress represents the wearer's wisdom and status in the tribe – the greater the variety of colour, the higher his level of spirituality.

The halo traditionally painted around or over the heads of saints by medieval artists also represented an aspect of the aura, depicting the exalted state, or even divinity, of the individual. The very fact that the artists painted the halo at all shows us that they must have been aware of the aura's existence, even though the subtle glow of golden light which they painted around the head is a mere part of an even greater whole. For the aura, when seen in its entirety, obscures the whole body with colour and movement, emanating outward from it into the surrounding space.

The tonsure of the monk (shaven head) was not some aberration which caught on amongst monastic communities, but was originally intended to fully expose both the crown chakra (Sahasrara), and the aura around the head, to God and cosmic influences.

How Does the Aura Manifest and Transmit?

First of all let us look at this from a spiritual point of view. Before the soul becomes embodied in flesh, it travels in its vibratory descent through the manifested worlds of the cosmos, drawing to itself along its way sheathes or bodies of energy. These sheathes enable the soul to function at the various levels to which it relates, and through which it descends, before eventually becoming encased, so to speak, in a physical body.

To enable the soul to exist in, and compete with, the alien circumstances in which it finds itself when housed in a physical body, it is necessary for it to be cosmically sustained, not only at a physical level, but also at the various other levels to which each of its other bodies relate. This need for cosmic sustenance necessitates the formation of a system of subtle psychic energy points whose vital job it is to control and modulate the inpouring cosmic energy. These points perform the function of small subtle transformers, modifying, transmuting and distributing the energy coming into the body (like electrical transformers stepping down a current of electricity) and maintaining man's equilibrium at all levels. These 'psychic transformers' are referred to in the Eastern traditions as 'chakras', which in Sanskrit means 'wheels' or 'circles', and they play an integral part in the evolution of man's consciousness. The role of the chakras will be discussed in Chapter Two.

We know, of course, that man is much more than just a physical body. The human organism is an electromagnetic unit of incredible power, assimilating and releasing energy, and is contained within its own spectrum of light and colour. In fact, man's subtle anatomy consists of seven vehicles or bodies of matter, and each vehicle is composed of a much finer material than the one below it, as they all rise in a gradually ascending vibratory scale, from the most dense (the physical body) to the purest and highest (the spirit). Man's bodies are of different degrees of density and expression and therefore allow the consciousness to manifest upon different planes, the physical body being of course the lowest form of expression.

The following analogy may help to illustrate this concept more fully. Consider for a few moments that you are observing molten wax being poured into a bowl of cold water. On entering the water the molten wax slowly solidifies to enable it to compete with the alien circumstances (the water) in which it finds itself. The liquid wax gradually solidifies, layer upon layer, rather like the soul on its downward vibratory descent through the manifested worlds of the cosmos, eventually to become embodied in a vehicle of flesh. Although this is a very simple analogy, it is, I feel, one that illustrates the concept perfectly well. For the soul, too, lives in an alien environment during its sojourn in this physical world. However, while it dwells here, the soul and its various subtle bodies of expression need to be constantly energized. Each of man's bodies radiates energy, and it is the energy radiating from *all* the seven bodies combined that constitutes the aura.

This beautiful, kaleidoscopic mass of colour is what sets man apart from all other living things. From a scientific as well as a metaphysical point of view, chemical energy created in the cells of the body undergoes an incredible process, during which it is quickly converted into light energy, culminating in the wonderful phenomenon of the aura. The actual luminous glow is scientifically referred to as the bioluminescence, from which a great deal of personal data is gleaned. I suppose one could say that the aura is one's personal database, containing past, present and future information about the individual's spiritual, physical, emotional and mental lives.

How do We Know the Aura Exists?

Modern technology has advanced to such an extent in this area that the aura can now actually be photographed in colour. The photographic technique presently employed in order to obtain these fascinating photographs is far superior to that initially developed by Semyon and Valentina Kirlian, a husband and wife team from Krasnodar near the Black Sea. They were the first people to photograph the aura with the sole intention of using the photographic method as a diagnostic tool. Some years ago 'screens' were developed, containing a special dye, which enabled the user, when looking through them, to 'see' the auric field. These screens were developed by Dr Walter Kilner, a radiologist at St Thomas's Hospital, London. Dr Kilner's extensive study of the human aura led him to write a book about it entitled *The Human Atmosphere*, later renamed *The Human Aura*. This book was, in fact, an inspiration to others working in the same field, and it also gave rise to further research on the human energy field. Kilner was reputed to be the first man to scientifically observe the aura and, as a result of his studies, many diseases can now be diagnosed and thus treated through the aura.

The aura certainly does not have to be seen for its existence to be felt. On the contrary, many people who work with the aura, in particular those working in the field of healing, develop a natural sensitivity to it. It is probably true to say that most healers can 'sense' the aura and, through their ability to sense it, will often find their hands drawn to the affected part of the body where healing is needed. This may be because the healer feels intense heat, or perhaps coldness around the troubled area, guiding them instinctively to the spot where treatment is needed.

However, whether or not you are a healer is immaterial, for sensing the aura is a phenomenon that most people have experienced, in one way or another, at some time in their lives, whether they know it or not. For example, you may be sitting in a theatre, or perhaps standing in a bus queue, when an uncomfortable, nagging feeling makes you turn round. On so doing, you catch the eye of someone who is staring intently at you. You can certainly 'feel' the person's eyes almost burning into the back of your head – that is why you turned round. Or you may perhaps have been alone in the house at some time, occupied with the housework, your attention on cleaning or tidying. You suddenly become convinced that someone is standing behind you, and you turn round quickly. Yet there is no one there, and the house remains quiet and empty. Or, again when you have been alone somewhere, either at home or in the office, you may suddenly have experienced an overwhelming smell of perfume or aftershave, which unexpectedly washes over your senses, reminding you of a dead relative or friend. All these phenomena are experienced through the medium of the aura.

What Subtle Energy is at Work?

In my studies of the aura I have found it to be more sensitive at a person's back, and in fact proportionately more extensive there, reaching further from the body than in the front. However, this does not seem to be the case with a visually handicapped person, where the aura tends to be equal in the distance it extends outwards all around the body. The absence of sight causes the aura at the front to be more developed than is the case with a sighted person. This extra development takes place in order to compensate for the absence of sight, and usually allows the sensitivity and awareness of the visually handicapped person to be heightened. In other words, the aura is our personal 'radar' system and, surrounding us completely, is constantly monitoring the surrounding environment and working relentlessly to warn us of approaching danger.

In a crowded theatre, for example, the aura usually contracts, forming a sort of protective shell around the person. However, once the individual feels relaxed and more comfortable sitting among strangers, the aura gradually expands to blend and thus merge with the collective auras of the rest of the audience. The combined energies of a crowd are quite a sight to behold. The beautiful display of varying colours constantly moves through an incredible sea of vibrant energy, swirling and pulsating, revealing, of course, the changing thought patterns, moods and emotions of all the people present.

How Can One Develop the Ability to 'See' the Aura?

It is important to understand that nearly all psychic phenomena experienced by man manifest, in one way or another, through the medium of the aura.

Learning to work with the aura is very important when endeavouring to cultivate any psychic potential. Once you have mastered the ability to control and expand your own aura, you will very quickly realize just what incredible power lies within. The more developed your auric skills become, the greater control you will have over your own life and the environment in which you live. Whether you actually 'see' or merely 'sense' the aura, this skill will enable you to 'read' others like an open book. The stronger your ability becomes, the more powerfully accurate your powers will be.

With the use of certain exercises and techniques the ability to see the aura can most certainly be developed. However, before any attempt is made to do so, it would be a good idea first of all to find out exactly what the aura looks like, and then you will know what it is you are looking for, and will, therefore, be able to identify it.

Most, if not all people, have seen an aspect of the aura at some time or another, even though they may have been completely unaware of it at the time. This is usually because, when the experience occurs, it is often dismissed as either a trick of the light, or perhaps put down to retina fatigue. For example, you may, on occasion, have been so engrossed in conversation with a friend that time has flown by, and you have failed to notice the sunlight fading and casting shadows across the room. Eventually your attention wanders for a moment, and at that point you may see a pale band of light around your friend's head. Of course, when you move your eyes to focus on it directly, it disappears. Out of the corner of your eye you may have seen a similar band of light around a chair, or even around a picture hanging on the wall. You would be forgiven for dismissing this phenomenon as a trick of the light or the result of tired eyes. After all, listening intently to what your friend has been saying will cause the optic lens to become fatigued. The subdued lighting, and the effort of your concentration, will put everything out of focus, causing the eyes to see things almost out of perspective. Difficult as it may be to believe, that pale band of light that you saw around your friend's head is actually an aspect of the aura. It became visible to you because your eyes were tired, and because of the subdued lighting.

One of the techniques used for developing the ability to see the aura is, in fact, the age-old art of scrying. Scrying has come to mean crystal gazing, although traditionally it is the ancient method of staring at any focal point with the sole intention of focusing the mind. The focal point can be anything from a crystal speculum to the flame of a lighted candle, or even a piece of quartz crystal placed in front of a lighted candle. Personally I would recommend the lighted-candle technique, as I have always found it to be the most effective when endeavouring to cultivate the image-making faculty. Remember, though, all these things are just tools with which to cultivate the consciousness. You may even find another method of scrying that suits you better. Some people prefer to gaze at a black bowl filled with water. As long as it works for you then use it.

Exercise 1

All you need for this exercise is a comfortable chair and a lighted candle. It often helps the concentration if you burn some incense and play some quiet, meditative music in the background.

- Light your candle and place it on a surface in front of you, as near to eyelevel as possible. Either lower the lights or turn them out completely, whichever you prefer.

- Sit comfortably in the chair, making sure that your chest, neck and head are as nearly in a straight line as possible, with your shoulders slightly back and your hands resting gently on your lap.

- Move your gaze slowly to the tip of the candle's flame and stare at it. Try not to blink or to move your eyes away from the flame, even for a moment.

- To aid your concentration and help you to relax, begin to

breathe deeply and slowly, allowing your stomach to rise as you breathe in, and then to fall as you breathe out, and so on.

- When you feel that you can no longer gaze at the flame without blinking (your eyes will begin to tear and you will need to blink to clear them), close your eyes very slowly. As you do so, place the palms of your hands over them, pressing very slightly on your eyeball.

- Within a few moments the after-image of the flame will gradually appear in your mind's eye.

- The whole object of the exercise is to hold the after-image of the flame in your mind's eye for as long as you can.

- Whilst holding it steady in your mind, continue to breathe in a slow and easy rhythm, ensuring that the inhalations and exhalations are fairly evenly spaced.

- You should notice that with each inhalation the image of the flame will grow stronger and more clearly defined on the screen of your mind. However, when the after-image eventually becomes fragmented and begins to fade, open your eyes, and very slowly return your gaze to the flame and repeat the whole process.

At first the exercise should be repeated only three or four times in one sitting, but when you feel comfortable with it, the number of repetitions should be increased to six or seven. In time, with practice and determination, you should find that the after-image of the flame will remain easily in the mind's eye, and will not fade until you allow it to do so. However, these results may not be achieved immediately, and it may take some time for the exercise to be mastered.

The benefits of this exercise can sometimes be quite startling. Not only does regular practice help to improve the concentration and cultivate one's ability to visualize, but your powers of observation will also improve. Practised over long periods of time, this exercise will stimulate the image-making faculty of the mind, precipitating the ability to 'see clearly'. It certainly helps to encourage any latent clairvoyant skills the practitioner may have, and makes one more visually sensitive to auric emanations. One cautionary note, however: it is advisable to remove contact lenses, if worn, before using this technique.

• •

Do not expect to see the aura immediately, but once it does become apparent to you, the exercise still needs to be practised to maintain and improve your perception of it. Even then, what you will probably be seeing is a minute aspect of an even greater whole. Seeing the aura opens up a whole new and extremely exciting aspect of the universe. In fact, seeing it is only the beginning, as the interpretation of the colours, their numerous shades, degrees and combinations varies widely among those who see, or who claim to see, the aura in its entirety.

It is important in your analysis of the aura that you do not allow yourself to be influenced by what others say that they see, but simply be guided by your own experience of what you yourself know you see. It is not my intention in this book to become embroiled in the debate over the interpretation of auric colours, as in my opinion this is very much a case of 'whatever works for you', and only practice and experience will help you along the way.

• •

Exercise 2

This is more a visual experiment than it is an exercise for training the mind. It will enable you to actually see exactly what the aura looks like so that you know what you are looking for.

• Slice a fresh red apple into four pieces and remove the dark brown pips. The pips must be dark brown, as opposed to white, as the dark colour is crucial to the experiment.

• Place a couple of pips on a piece of white paper and stare at them for a few moments. Try not to let your gaze wander, as this merely defeats the object of the whole exercise.

• In a very short time you will begin to see a faint glow around the outline of the pips – a sort of pale blue vapour, which will seem to move around the pips in a clockwise motion.

• The longer you stare at the pips the stronger the vaporous glow around them will become.

• What you are actually seeing is the aura of the pips, i.e. the energy radiating from them. This energy represents their strength and vitality, synonymous with the 'health' aura.

• As you continue to watch the aura moving around the pips, you will gradually begin to see fine streams of energy emanating from them. These streams of energy represent the consistency of the vitality present in the pips, and their general condition.

- Move the pips about an inch apart, and you will see the energy radiating from each one towards the other, until they appear to blend perfectly.

- For the next part of the experiment place the same pips in an envelope and put them to one side, preferably in a dry, dark place, for 24 hours.

- After the suggested period, remove the pips from the envelope and place them once again on a white piece of paper.

- Now, remove some more pips from a fresh apple, and then place these alongside the old pips, and watch what happens.

- You will notice that the vaporous glow around the old pips will not appear quite as vibrant and bright, in comparison to the energy radiating from the fresh pips. The streams of energy that were apparent when the pips were fresh will now appear to be slowly fading, in much the same way as the energy seen radiating from a sick or dying person.

- Wait a few minutes longer to see an incredible phenomenon occur. You will soon see the energy radiating from the fresh pips gradually begin to stream towards the dry, dying pips, in a concerted effort to revitalize them. For a while the older pips may appear to recover, but this recovery is transitory, and eventually they will wither and die.

● ●

The object of this experiment is not only to let you see exactly what the aura looks like, but also to show you just how a healthy aura, full of vitality, can positively affect an unhealthy one lacking such vitality. This process of 'passing on' energy should be of great interest to those endeavouring to develop the ability to heal, and should demonstrate the mechanics of psychic healing. Although, strictly speaking, this book is not concerned with the development of healing skills, I will be covering the concept of *energy*, and how it is used during the process of psychic development, in Chapter Three. I have included some useful tips on how best to control this energy, something that should be extremely beneficial to any aspiring healer.

As I have mentioned above, most if not all psychic abilities manifest in one way or another through the medium of the aura, and it is through the aura that subtle vibrations are transmitted and received. However, I must point out that the aura is a sort of radar device and not a distinct faculty.

How many times have you been thinking about someone from whom you haven't heard for a while and, only a short time later, they telephone you, or even knock on your door? This might, of course, be put down to coincidence or chance but, more often than not, it is the result of telepathy, or mind-to-mind communication – perfect resonance between two people.

If we work on the premise that 'thoughts are living things', then it certainly makes sense to accept that those thoughts are capable of being projected, either consciously or otherwise, almost instantaneously, from one place to another, unrestricted by time or space. In fact, a small experiment can easily prove this.

• •

Exercise 3

- Ask a friend to sit quietly in another room, with a pencil and paper to hand. Tell them to close their eyes and wait until they feel inspired to draw something.

- Sit quietly by yourself with your eyes closed. Think of a

shape, a word or an object. Build up the image of whatever you have chosen very clearly in your mind, and then slowly transmit it to your friend in the adjacent room.

- The most effective method of transmitting pictures is to precede the transmission with some gentle, slow, rhythmic breathing, projecting your picture on each exhalation. In this way the rhythm of the telepathic process is consistently maintained, which is important to affect positive results. Do not be disappointed if the experiment proves unsuccessful at first. On occasion, a rapport with your partner has to be established before clear mental images can be successfully transmitted and received. Although telepathic communication can sometimes be quite spontaneous, the ability usually needs to be worked at and developed. Of course, as is the case with everything, practice and determination always produce positive, successful results. Once the telepathic flow has been successfully achieved the receiver will see the pictures very clearly in their mind, just as in our first exercise when you saw the after-image of the flame of the candle.

- A frequent mistake is for the receiver to question the pictures, which they see floating through their consciousness. Try not to stop, think and question, as this will interfere with any successful transmission. It is important to respond immediately to the impressions that float into the mind by drawing them, and thus acknowledge receipt.

As with all psychic impressions, telepathic images can be fleeting, and will be strengthened only through an immediate response. Once psychic images have been successfully transmitted and received, the transmitter should have a turn at receiving. Only when seven or more transmissions have been successfully received consistently, over a period of a week or more, can one safely regard the telepathic exercise as successful.

• •

I mentioned earlier the importance of learning to work with the aura. To this end you will find the following exercises invaluable.

• •

Exercise 4a

The ability to expand and contract your aura is a skill that, in fact, comes quite naturally without any great effort to everyone.

• You will need to work with a partner. Choose someone with whom you feel comfortable. You will also need a pair of divining rods. Should you not be able to obtain these, they are quite simple to make. Cut two lengths of wire, approximately 15–18in (37–45cm) in length, from two wire coat hangers. Bend each piece into an 'L' shape.

• Take one wire rod in each hand and, gripping them loosely by the short length, point them in front of you. When the divining rods locate a source of energy, they will either cross over each other or turn away from each other.

• Ask your partner to hide an object, and then mentally tell your divining rods to locate it – and see what happens.

• Hold the rods in front of you and allow them to lead you. Try to be aware of any sensations you may feel in your hands. You may experience tingling or even some vibration.

- It may take some time to familiarize yourself with your divining rods but, with a little patience and practice, results will most definitely be achieved.

Exercise 4b

- Ask your partner to stand with their back against the wall.

- Stand facing them at a distance of at least 6ft (approximately 182cm).

- Holding the divining rods in front of you, pointing towards your partner, walk slowly towards them until the rods either cross over or move apart. The point at which the rods move is where your partner's aura begins.

- Repeat the exercise but, this time, ask your partner to stand facing the wall. Again from some distance, begin to approach them slowly, stopping when the rods begin to move. This time you should notice that the point at which the rods begin to move will be considerably further away from your partner, showing that the aura at the rear is proportionately greater, extending further out from the body, than at the front.

- Change places and ask your partner to 'home in' on you with the divining rods. Compare the difference in aura sizes.

Exercise 4c

- Ask your friend to repeat the exercise, homing in on you with the divining rods, but this time close your eyes and cover your ears to block out any sound. Before your friend

moves towards you he or she should stand quietly for a
few moments in order to create in you a feeling of
anticipation. This feeling of uncertainty, and possible
apprehension, actually causes the aura to expand in
anticipation of the approaching danger.

• The aura's expansion will be apparent in the movement of
the divining rods. Repeat the experiment, this time with
your back to your partner, and note just how much your
aura expands.

Practising this method at least twice a day will enable you to
master the ability to control and project your auric energies.
The benefits will enhance your everyday life, as well as your
psychic work, and will certainly strengthen your personality,
making you more positive in everything you do.

• •

As one can exercise the physical body to improve its muscle tone
and strength, the mind can also be exercised to enhance its performance and overall efficiency, and to cultivate psychic skills.
Near the end of this book (Chapter Eleven), I will examine
different types of meditation that are specially designed to improve
such skills, to heighten your awareness of the aura, and so infuse it
with vitality. Meditation *must*, without a doubt, play an extremely
important part in the development and ultimate cultivation of the
psychic faculties, and it should be used in your personal daily
programme.

Chapter Two

Activating the Chakras

There are varying, conflicting ideas as to what chakras are, and what part they actually play in the manifestation of consciousness. And although I have endeavoured to present them in an easy-to-understand way, I do hope that you will still appreciate their importance in the process of psychic development, and will find what I have written useful in your endeavours.

Man is an extremely complex being, and is much more than just a physical body. In fact, he is a veritable powerhouse of energy, encased within a vibratory spectrum of numerous sheathes or bodies, each one composed of a much finer material than the one below it.

The whole of man's subtle anatomy is permeated by a complex network of etheric wiring or channels along which energy is conveyed to the organs of the physical body, thereby maintaining the body's equilibrium on all levels of consciousness. All this energy is controlled, so to speak, by a complex system of subtle energy centres which, as I have mentioned, are called chakras (from the Sanskrit meaning 'wheels' or 'circles').

It is the primary purpose of this chapter to explain how your psychic abilities work, and to show you that it is possible to improve those abilities simply by increasing the activity of your chakras. I always use the analogy of the motor mechanic and the engine. You have the ability to improve the performance of the chakras simply by understanding how it all works and knowing exactly what is required to maintain order in the subtle anatomy.

The chakras appear to be connected in some way to the endocrine glands and nerve plexuses, through an extensive system of channels, the Sanskrit word for which is *nadis*. The word nadi means 'nerve', only at a more subtle level, and it is along these nadis that energy flows from the chakras to the organs of the physical body. Chakras are in some way responsible for the distribution of energy and for the development and evolution of man's consciousness. Some esoteric schools of thought believe that the chakra system is also some type of *memory bank*, within which is stored experience data from the present and previous incarnations. They represent the various degrees of man's consciousness, and although all the chakras are potentially present at birth, only one can be seen to be fully functioning at that time. The others take a full seven-year cycle before activity becomes apparent.

Literally hundreds of extremely minor chakras permeate man's subtle anatomy. There are major and minor vortices of energy, modifying and distributing the incoming force, and maintaining a well-balanced individual in body, mind and soul.

However, there are seven major chakras that are considered primary, and these are to be seen across the surface of the etheric body, in the spinal column. They are perceived as saucer-like impressions, having the appearance of small flowers whose petals increase in number as they ascend the spine.

The first chakra to be awakened, at birth, is called *Muladhara* and is situated at the base of the spine. This extremely important centre limits the new-born baby's awareness to the instinctive level, and is, in fact, responsible for all its babyish actions, from crying to be fed, to reaching instinctively for its mother's breast.

Thus, the chakras open in sequence, at the rate of one a year, beginning with the one at the base of the spine, and concluding the cycle (when the child is 7 years old) with the chakra on the crown of the head, called *Sahasrara*.

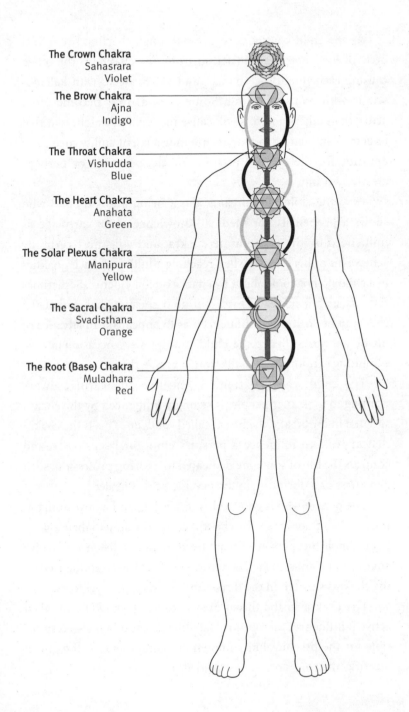

The Crown Chakra
Sahasrara
Violet

The Brow Chakra
Ajna
Indigo

The Throat Chakra
Vishudda
Blue

The Heart Chakra
Anahata
Green

The Solar Plexus Chakra
Manipura
Yellow

The Sacral Chakra
Svadisthana
Orange

The Root (Base) Chakra
Muladhara
Red

As the child continues to grow through the first seven-year cycle of life, energy is transferred from one chakra to the other, causing each one to be vivified, and to coruscate with kaleidoscopic whirlpools of colour. Some chakras may become more active than others and this will cause the child's awareness at that level to be influenced, often precipitating a latent ability such as an aptitude for the creative arts, i.e. music, painting, or perhaps creative writing.

Even the child who dreams about being a doctor, and who shows a propensity for medical knowledge at an early age, is influenced by the appropriate chakra, and will most certainly achieve his or her dreams when reaching adulthood. Such qualities in a child do not come about by chance or coincidence. Sometimes there is such a powerful force within a specific chakra that the child can be so strongly influenced as to appear far in advance of his or her years; hence the child prodigies we occasionally see exhibiting extraordinary skills from a very early age.

The child who is extremely sensitive and caring, always wanting to look after people, is strongly influenced by the chakra situated in the area of the heart, called *Anahata*. This is the chakra that appears to influence a person's emotional sensitivity, and controls the life of someone dedicated to a caring profession, such as a nurse or a doctor or, in the psychic field, a healer.

The person who is good at his or her job, and enjoys doing it, is strongly influenced by the chakras corresponding to their ability. For example, the person who has been trained to listen and to give advice, and who is, in fact, extremely good at this, is influenced by the chakras situated in the throat and between the eyebrows.

The chakra in the throat area is called *Vishudda* and when active it influences the auditory faculties. Vishudda is also responsible for the psychic ability known as clairaudience – the gift of 'hearing' the voices of the so-called 'dead'.

The chakra between the eyebrows is called *Ajna* and is responsible for the ability to 'see'. Anyone who is extremely observant and notices detail is influenced by Ajna. This chakra is situated in the seat of the traditional 'third eye', and is responsible for the psychic ability known as clairvoyance.

It is important to note, however, that a psychic ability such as clairvoyance or clairaudience will only manifest through the appropriate chakra when the second and third chakras have also been activated. These chakras, *Svadisthana* and *Manipura*, together form an integral part of man's subtle anatomy. Manipura is associated with the solar plexus, or, in yogic parlance, the 'Sun Centre', and is the powerhouse of all of man's psychic abilities.

Everything said so far will most probably be academic, so, to enable you to have a fairly good working idea that the chakras *do* exist, I would like you to experience them for yourself. With the help of a few simple experiments you can become more aware of the chakras, and will be able to use them to your advantage.

· ·

Exercise 5

For this experiment you will need to enlist the help of a partner.

• Stand up straight, with your right arm extended in front of you. Allow your partner (using one hand) to gently push your arm down, but resist their pressure just enough to make it clear to them how much

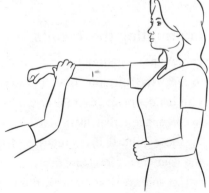

strength you possess in your arm. You will need to know this for purposes of comparison later. Having done this, rest your arm for a moment.

- Repeat the process. However, this time, while your partner is applying pressure to your right arm, place your left hand over your area of Muladhara (the genital area). Make a note of any changes in the strength of your right arm. Rest your arm.

- Repeat the process. This time, place your left hand gently over the area of Svadisthana (over your navel). Again, make a note of any changes to the strength of your right arm. Rest your arm.

- Repeat the process. Move your left hand to the area of Manipura, immediately below the left-hand side of the rib cage, slightly above the navel. Make a note of any changes in the strength of your right arm, as your partner applies a little pressure to it. Rest your arm.

- Repeat the process, working your way through all seven chakras, from the base chakra to the crown chakra, noting their condition as you go.

Interpreting the Results

I always use this simple muscle-testing experiment as it allows you to check the condition of each chakra. If your arm feels weak when your hand is placed over the area of the first chakra (Muladhara) this would suggest that little activity is present at that point. It will therefore indicate that you are perhaps currently a little run-down and your energy levels are depleted. However, should your right arm exhibit an increase of strength, this would be indicative of a great deal of vitality and stamina and also that you are extremely intuitive.

Should the second and third chakras show signs of weakness or underactivity (Svadisthana and Manipura), this would indicate that you are a nervy person, perhaps a little too sensitive or lacking in confidence. However, if they exhibit a surge of strength, this will reveal your inner strength and confidence, and your ability to cope in times of stress and crisis. The fourth chakra (Anahata) reveals the balance of your life. Should it show signs of weakness or inactivity, this would indicate emotional insecurity, sadness, and lack of confidence. However, should Anahata prove to be strong when pressure is applied to your right arm, this would reveal stability, warmth, compassion and control of the emotions.

If weakness is exhibited in the throat area or fifth chakra (Vishudda), this would indicate that you are sluggish, slow to respond, do not pay attention and find it difficult to concentrate for any length of time. However, should strength be found in that area, you are probably versatile, resourceful, creative and observant. It would also mean that psychic abilities are inherent, and that this psychic centre is open to the impulses of the supersensual universe.

Should the sixth chakra (Ajna) appear weak when pressure is applied to your extended right arm, you lack the ability to concentrate, and you probably do not overtax your imagination. In fact, you probably lack imagination and drive, and have no real ambition or deep interest in anything in particular. You may also suffer from frequent headaches, due to an insufficient flow of energy into the chakra. However, should Ajna appear strong, you are most certainly observant, you notice detail, your senses are very sharp and you possess psychic potential.

While Sahasrara, the crown chakra, is largely neutral in all people, at least at this stage of evolution, its very existence connects man to God and the cosmos, determining his spiritual status and orientation to self-knowledge. This chakra plays an important part in man's spiritual evolution, so it cannot therefore be influenced to any great degree.

• •

Exercise 6

Not only does this exercise infuse the chakras with vitality and power, but it also nearly always produces feelings of general wellbeing as a result. It has the effect of almost washing one's aura with a powerful surge of energy, thus heightening one's general awareness.

- You will need a piece of amethyst crystal and a piece of clear quartz crystal, both small enough to hold comfortably in your hands. Amethyst, known as the spiritual stone, possesses calming qualities that affect the emotions and nervous system, as well as encouraging heightened states of spiritual awareness. Clear quartz is an energy enhancer, increasing the energy and power in anything placed close to it. It has the effect of clearing the mind and sharpening the senses.

- Sitting comfortably with your back straight, take the piece of amethyst in your right hand and the clear quartz in your left hand, and sit quietly with your eyes closed and both hands on your lap.

- Remain in this position until the mind has become quiet. Place your right hand, holding the piece of amethyst, gently on top of your head. Place your left hand, holding the piece of clear quartz, at the base of your spine.

- Remain in this position until you feel the temperature change in your right hand on top of your head. At this

point swap your hands around, and place your left hand
(with the quartz) on top of your head, and your right hand
(with the amethyst) at the base of your spine.

- Continue to repeat the exercise until both hands have
rested on the head at least ten times. Then sit quietly for a
further ten minutes with your eyes closed, allowing the
energy to circulate around your body. If you have practised
the exercise correctly you may even feel your spine,
forehead and hands tingling. You may also experience a
feeling of disorientation as though you have breathed in
fresh mountain air.

There are many benefits to be gained from this 'infusing'
method. It is also effective in promoting calmness and
serenity, and in easing pain. Twenty minutes after you have
completed this exercise repeat Exercise 5. Make a note of
any significant changes in the results. If you can see a marked
improvement in the activity in your chakras there will be little
need for you to use any other method of chakra activation,
unless of course you do not feel comfortable with this
particular exercise.

It would also be a good idea to read through the instructions
a few times before attempting the exercise. Fix the process
clearly in your mind so that you feel confident in what you are
trying to achieve.

Exercise 7

Sit in a comfortable chair for five to ten minutes, until the mind becomes quiet. Now shake your hands vigorously, until you can feel your fingers tingle.

• Place your fingers gently on your solar plexus and breathe in slowly and deeply. As you do so, imagine that you are breathing in a stream of pure white light through your nostrils, down into your solar plexus, and out into your fingertips.

• When you have taken a complete breath, hold it, and slowly transfer your fingertips to your forehead.

• Gently touching the area between your eyebrows slowly expel your breath, imagining that you are breathing the pure white light out through your fingertips, filling your head completely with the light.

• When your breath has been fully expelled, hold it, and return your fingertips to your solar plexus, breathing the white light in once again.

• Repeat the process, but this time move your fingertips slowly to the throat area, expelling the white light through your fingertips and filling your throat with vitality and energy. When your breath has been fully expelled, return your fingertips to the solar plexus.

• Repeat the process. This time transfer your fingertips slowly to the heart area, flooding the heart chakra completely with white light. When your breath and the white light have been fully expelled, return your fingertips slowly to the solar plexus.

- Repeat the whole process down to the genital area, flooding each chakra completely with energy and vitality. When you have completed the process, and your breath and the white light have been fully expelled, breathe in and out quickly, ballooning your cheeks, and blowing through your lips with each exhalation. At the same time sweep your open hands up and down the front of your face, chest and stomach areas. Do this four or five times, and then sit quietly for five minutes, imbibing the moving energy that will appear to be vibrating through your whole body.

As the crown chakra is neutral in the majority of people it is not included in this exercise. Sahasara becomes active in sync with the evolution of the individual's spiritual consciousness; it is therefore not necessary to precipitate it with the use of this exercise.

This is an extremely invigorating exercise, and one that you will find beneficial in activating the main chakras. To gain the most benefit from it, however, the exercise should be practised morning and evening.

• •

In theory, the movements of the chakras should alternate from clockwise to anticlockwise down the body, beginning with the brow chakra, which itself should move with a clockwise motion. The base chakra should show an anticlockwise motion, concluding the alternating sequence. Incidentally, the chakra system of women is usually the opposite way around, starting with an anticlockwise movement at the brow chakra, and concluding with a clockwise motion in the base chakra.

Although it is believed that a healthy, well-balanced person should have a correctly aligned vibratory chakra system with alternating movements, this may not always be the case, because the chakras do change polarity throughout the day. This change may occur as a result of fatigue, stress, concentration, diet, etc. Nonetheless, there is no reason why the chakras cannot be stimulated into activity and controlled by using the methods given here.

Incidentally, there is little use in dowsing (i.e. using a pendulum or dowsing rods to locate an energy source) the crown chakra, as I have always found this to be unaffected by such treatments. In any case, the chakras with which we should be mostly concerned are, in fact, those that are associated directly with one's psychic abilities. Although the crown chakra is an extremely important chakra, especially where the evolution of man's spiritual consciousness is concerned, it is my belief that it should not be included when considering, or carrying out, activation of the chakras, due to its sensitive and vulnerable nature. The crown chakra slowly evolves according to the rate of one's own spiritual development, and represents, on a more subtle level, man's spiritual consciousness.

• •

Exercise 8

For this experiment you will need to work with a partner again. You will also require five small pieces of clear quartz crystal and a pendulum – preferably a crystal one, as these are more effective where chakra work is concerned.

- First, lie flat on the floor, using a cushion to support your head. Your partner should place one quartz crystal beside each of your heels, one next to each shoulder, and one as

close to the crown of the head as possible. Your partner
will now dowse your chakras, using the pendulum,
beginning with the brow chakra.

- The pendulum should be held as steadily as possible over
  the chakra at a distance of approximately 2in (5cm), until
  some movement has been affected in it. The amount of
  movement in the pendulum, which will rotate either
  clockwise or anticlockwise, will in fact signify how much
  activity is present in the chakra.

- Dowse all the chakras in sequence, making a note of their
  condition so that you can chart any improvement.

- At the conclusion of the exercise, continue to lie in the
  same position, with your hands resting lightly over the
  solar plexus, for at least 20 minutes. Breathe in a slow
  and rhythmical manner, making sure that the inhalations
  and exhalations are evenly spaced.

- Imagine powerful white energy swirling around you,
  passing through your body, from one crystal to the other.

- Visualize this energy moving through each of your
  chakras, and mentally see each chakra pulsating and
  glowing.

- Spend a few minutes on each chakra, and mentally see
  them vivified and coruscating with vibrant energy.

It is not enough to merely imagine the chakras coming alive
with colour and vitality, for these surges of energy must also
be 'felt' and 'experienced' through your imagination.
Remember, you are dealing with subtle energy forces, over
which the mind has a greater influence than does the physical
body. This energy needs to be visualized, focused on and

mentally controlled in order to achieve the most effective and positive results.

It is quite usual to feel extremely tired when the exercise is over. It is important that a period of rest be taken now to enable positive results to be achieved.

There would be little use in dowsing the chakras again immediately after the exercise, because time is needed for the energy to circulate through the system, and for the results to be seen. When you feel fully refreshed your partner should dowse the chakras once more, repeating the same process and recording any changes in activity in the chakras.

The mouth can often feel quite parched as a result of this exercise, so drink a glass of fresh, clear water when the whole treatment has been completed. Before consuming the water, pour it from one vessel to another, backwards and forwards through the air, in order to revitalize it with the force known as *prana*. We will discuss this important energy in the next chapter.

• •

Chapter Three

Psychic Energy and Thought Power

Most people have only a superficial contact with the world in which they live, and are largely oblivious to the life that surrounds them. Developing your psychic powers will allow you to gain access to a whole new and beautiful dimension of the universe, thus making each and every experience seem like an exciting and mysterious adventure.

We are influenced in more ways than one by the world which surrounds us, and we become what and who we are as a result of the knowledge we acquire of it. We experience this world through our five senses, and should any of these senses be defective in any way whatsoever, then the knowledge and experience we have of this world would be greatly lessened as a direct consequence.

Our five senses are active all the time, enabling us to see, hear, touch, taste and smell the objects of the world in which we live. However, you very rarely realize what complex processes of consciousness are actually involved in your awareness of the world that surrounds you. Nor do you realize that you know only an extremely minute part of what exactly there is to know! Once the psychic faculties have been awakened and cultivated, you will be able to gain access to an abundance of information about the world – and will then be able to 'read' objects and people as easily as reading a book. Needless to say, once this has been achieved you will be able to gain greater control of your life.

Personally, I do not subscribe to the old saying 'A little knowledge is a dangerous thing'. On the contrary, it is, I believe, your obligation to search and obtain what knowledge you can. I would say that a little knowledge is certainly far better than none, that is, as long as it is correct, and it works for you.

Whatever your reason for wanting to develop psychic powers, the responsibility for such a profound transformation ultimately lies with you. You must therefore fully understand its broader implications and innumerable possibilities. Once development begins to take place, nothing in your life will ever quite be the same again. The whole concept of your life will change quite dramatically, and the emotional highs and lows that you experienced in the past will be a mere shadow of the highs and lows you will experience in the future. It is a fallacy to believe that psychic powers will exempt you from pain and suffering simply because you are privy to knowledge that is denied to others. I am often reminded of the wise words of the 19th-century mystic and dramatist, Maurice Maeterlinck.

> *The wise man too must suffer, and suffering forms a*
> *constituent part of his wisdom. He shall suffer in the*
> *flesh, in the heart and in the soul. And being nearer to*
> *mankind – no, being nearer to God as ever the wise*
> *man must be, the sufferings of others are his, in that his*
> *nature is far more complete than his brothers.*

Let us now consider 'thought power' and the concept of *psychic energy*. Psychic powers are all concerned with learning to control and direct such energy.

The word *prana* is used in Eastern philosophy to describe all energy in the universe. Prana is in fact the subtle agent through which the life of the body is sustained, and is therefore the principle responsible for the maintenance of life in the physical body. It integrates the cells into a whole, and animates the body. Prana is all-pervading, and is to be found in everything having life, and of course, everything possesses life to some greater or lesser degree. Although prana is in the air that we breathe it is not the air itself. It is found working through all forms of matter, but it is not matter itself. It is in the water that we drink, and is taken in by the animal and the plant kingdoms. Although prana exists in all these things, it is, in fact, completely independent of them.

When the physical body is depleted in prana, illness or disease results. Should prana cease to be present in the physical body, death would immediately occur. It must, therefore, be understood that prana has a specific part to play in the manifestation of life, apart from the obvious physiological function, and is, therefore, responsible for it.

Prana is such a dynamic force that to be aware of its very existence alone is to be more than halfway to gaining control of its universal power. It sustains and perpetuates the life in everything, and gives force and power to our thoughts and the way in which we think. It can infuse life into our thoughts, and enables us to propel them in any direction we choose, distance no object, for of course *thoughts are living things*. The stronger the thought, the more energy with which we charge that thought. The more energy present with each thought, the longer that thought will persist in the psychic space.

This concept was known to the ancient Egyptians, who utilized this powerful force to create concentrations of energy to protect the tombs of their great kings. These forces are probably still in existence today, silently protecting those tombs still as yet undiscovered.

Working on the premise that 'thoughts are living things', the thoughts we create with a specific mission in mind are automatically infused with prana, which propels them to do our bidding.

Most of the thoughts that are discharged during the course of the day however, such as 'What shall I cook for dinner?', 'It looks like rain,' or even, 'I'll have to pick the children up from school,' have little or no force behind them. They dissipate and are then absorbed by the psychic space, to be resolved back into the ether. But those strong emotions which constantly occupy our thoughts, whether with fear or joy, happiness or sadness, love or hate, are immediately enveloped and infused with streams of prana, propelling them and lending them wings.

We are continually peopling our own private portion in space by the way we think, and we are constantly being pulled along by those concentrations of thoughts which we have created previously. As a direct consequence, nature always works towards the gratification of our most secret desires. We are in fact the architects of our own destinies by the way we think. You only have to look at how difficult it is to pull yourself out of depression, and to be more positive when problems have crowded in upon you. When things go wrong in your life it is very difficult, if not impossible, to fight back against circumstances. However, before your circumstances can ever change, you must transform the way you think. This is the great Law of Attraction. Smile at the universe and the universe will smile at you! What you send out into the universe will come back tenfold. This is the Law of Attraction in operation, a law which is both right and just!

This concept applies not only to the spiritual life, but also to the mental, moral and physical lives. Once you are able to comprehend the fundamental principles underlying the concept of psychic energy and the power of thought, it is easy to see exactly what powers lie within you.

During the course of a normal day you probably touch thousands of objects without being aware of it. Things around the home and in the workplace, which are handled and touched by you, therefore possess tiny particles of your personal energies – minute particles of you. Although these things are only superficially encountered, and are probably therefore 'overprinted' with the vibrations of many other people, personal items such as jewellery, clothing, even domestic objects, may be strongly impregnated with your own energies.

By simply holding a personal item belonging either to someone living, or perhaps to someone who has long since died, it is possible to psychically 'read' its vibratory history, rather like flicking through the pages of a book. Although it takes time to perfect such a skill, I know of no more effective method of cultivating the psychic ability of clairvoyance. This method of 'reading' articles is called 'psychometry'; an extremely precise method of divination, favoured by many clairvoyants and psychic readers. Although, strictly speaking, psychometry can only be used to glean information pertaining to the past and present of those to whom the articles belong, or have belonged, I have known the information thus obtained to be extremely accurate.

On occasions, psychometry can be used as a 'bridge', so to speak, to enable the reader to make contact with someone in the *spirit world* and to give concrete evidence of that person's continued existence.

A psychic will often ask a 'sitter' to hand them an item of personal jewellery to use as a sort of focal point, primarily to help them make a connection with that person. Quite often the information given by the psychic does not come from the item of jewellery, and may, in fact, have nothing whatsoever to do with it. But there are others who rely solely upon their ability to 'psychometrize', and without this skill they may find that they can do nothing. This, however, is down to training rather than to their lack of ability.

Psychometry not only helps to heighten one's sensitivity to

the vibratory atmosphere of objects and people, it is also extremely effective in the development and cultivation of concentration, and this is a prerequisite where psychic work is concerned.

Psychometry is an ideal tool, and a useful and very effective means of improving one's psychic ability. However, one should not come to depend upon it totally. Use it, by all means, but use it along with other methods and as an integral part of your daily training programme. Once you have mastered the technique of using psychometry as a means of mentally processing information from a solid object, you should eventually find that you will quickly be able to 'home in' on things and people with great ease, without any physical contact at all.

Exercise 9

- Ask your friends to bring along some items of jewellery belonging to people you have not known.

- Before you begin, sit quietly for a few minutes, until your mind is calm and you feel quite relaxed.

- Ask someone to hand you an article, and hold it gently in your fingertips. At first, do not try to achieve anything other than allowing your mind to blend with the article in your hand.

- Use both hands, and as many fingers as possible in the exercise.

- When you feel calm and your mind is quiet, try to feel that you have almost become the article, and completely blended with it.

- Examine all its qualities – its weight, texture, shape, even its temperature. You may not have any control over the mental impressions that pass spontaneously through your mind. Should this be the case, mentally process them and say aloud what you see or feel, allowing a friend to write down exactly what you say.

- It is extremely important not to question or analyse too deeply everything that comes into your mind. The impression may be fleeting and may even be just vague images or feelings. You may even sense fragrance wafting over you, or see a sequence of symbols passing through your mind. Psychometry can produce anything and everything, and so you must be mentally prepared.

- Should the flow of impressions cease, mentally ask the article questions, for example: 'To whom did the ring or watch belong?' Or, 'Where and when was it bought?' Or even, 'Are they dead? And if so how did they die?' Ask the article for dates and descriptions. Try to be adventurous with your questions. After all, you have nothing to lose and everything to gain.

- When you feel quite confident practising psychometry, it will be as easy as reading a book, and you may feel sufficiently competent to take your time when mentally processing the data that can sometime flash very quickly through your mind.

Do not make this experiment laborious; trying to force psychometry to work merely defeats the object of the whole exercise. If nothing comes to you it may well be that you need to try a different article. This may sound hard to believe, but some articles – like people – refuse to say anything. Experiment with as many different objects as possible. Some people condition themselves into believing that they can only psychometrize certain objects – even objects of a particular size. This is a fallacy: once the ability has been developed to use psychometry as a means of psychically processing data from artefacts, then any object of any size may be used in the psychic analysis.

. . . .

Remember – psychometry is merely a useful tool, albeit an effective one. Although it can certainly produce very accurate information, once you have mastered the ability you will realize that you are most certainly capable of achieving much more.

Should you achieve positive results from psychometry and, therefore, feel comfortable enough to include it in your training programme, I believe it would be a good idea to also include a scrying technique – which will encourage your psychic visual response mechanism to develop.

Although often treated with cynicism and disdain, I strongly recommend that you obtain a good-quality crystal speculum (crystal ball) to aid you in your training programme. It is true to say that crystal balls usually conjure up ideas of a mysterious Gypsy Rose Lee figure sitting in a booth in a seaside resort, but I would ask you not to discount it as a possibility. The crystal ball has been an effective method of divination, used by seers for thousands of years. If it worked for them it can certainly work for you.

. . . .

Exercise 10

- Having placed your crystal speculum comfortably upon its pedestal, stand it on a table over which you should have placed a covering of black velvet. This helps to reduce any light reflection, making it easier to concentrate.

- The lighting in the room should be subdued, and try to create a pleasant atmosphere, perhaps by burning some sweet-smelling incense with some background music.

- Having set the scene, sit as comfortably as possible, with the crystal speculum as close to eyelevel as is necessary.

- Simply gaze at the crystal speculum, ignoring any particles of light that may have filtered onto the surface of the crystal.

- At first it is important not to blink, or to move your eyes away from the crystal even for a moment. Try not to be distracted as your eyes inevitably begin to move out of focus.

- When you feel that you can no longer stare at the crystal speculum without clearing your eyes, very slowly close them. Sit for a few moments, allowing the after-image of the crystal to come into your mind's eye.

- Continuing to sit quietly, attune your mind to the crystal, sending the thoughts to it, 'Allow me to see; allow me to see clearly.'

- By mentally interacting in this way with the crystal speculum, you initiate the programming process, thus allowing a connection between you and the crystal to be fully established.

- Once your mind has become completely relaxed and attuned to the vibrations of the crystal ball, open your eyes and return your gaze to it. As with the previous exercise, do not make this a labour, or you will merely defeat the object of the exercise, which is, of course, to see astral images more clearly.

- Continue to gaze at the crystal speculum, blinking to clear your eyes when necessary. Try not to think of any one particular thing, or allow your thoughts to wander from the crystal.

- At this point, *beware*! It is the time when most people become a little impatient, thinking that nothing is going to happen. But with crystal gazing, more than any other form of divination, a patient, determined attitude is definitely needed, and your patience will most certainly be rewarded with some startling results.

- Eventually, the interior of the crystal ball will appear to sparkle with a sort of green effervescence, full of movement and light. This will gradually subside, giving way to a slowly descending dark shadow which, as it falls, will cover the crystal ball completely.

- Your patience will be tested at this point, as the shadow may remain there, over the crystal ball, for quite some time. However, if you restrain your impatience and simply continue to watch, the shadow, or 'dark veil' as it is often called, will eventually begin to rise, uncovering the illuminated crystal speculum, leaving it bright and alive. At first you will see nothing, although there will appear to be bright light shining from within the very heart of the crystal speculum.

- Eventually, pictures will appear in the crystal ball – landscapes, faces, and often beautiful colours. These images will have no great significance at first, and will not be familiar to you. It will take some time for your astral vision to be developed, but in the meantime you must not allow yourself to become disheartened, and must continue to practise with the crystal speculum as often as time will permit.

- Even though the images you see at first in the crystal ball will probably have no meaning to you, you will still find them fascinating and it will be just like watching a film on the television.

- Also, whilst gazing at the crystal ball it is quite common for the gazer to see images and light forms in their peripheral field of vision. These forms may sometimes appear to dance about you, but as soon as you move your eyes from the crystal to look at them, they simply disappear.

Exercise 11

Once the art of scrying has been mastered, and you feel quite confident that it is working for you, you may like to try reading the crystal speculum for someone else, preferably a friend.

- Ask the person to hold the crystal ball gently in their hands for a few moments, moving it up to touch their forehead as they make a few wishes or silent requests. Take the ball from them and return it to its pedestal. With your hands still cupped around it, begin to gaze at the crystal ball as you did for yourself.

- You may find that pictures appear almost immediately, without any effervescence or dark veil, or you may have to go through the whole procedure again. Whatever the case, once the art has been mastered, I guarantee that you will be pleased with the results.

- Remember – the art of scrying can take some time to develop. You may be one of the lucky ones, however, and be fortunate enough to obtain positive results almost immediately.

A sensitive person is certainly far more susceptible to the subtle impulses of a psychically charged atmosphere than a nonsensitive person. Such sensitive people may often find themselves being constantly, and unknowingly, invaded by invisible psychic forces. However, not all of those invisible forces are of a negative nature. On the contrary, the sensitive person is also open to the influencing powers of positive, loving energies, also created, like the negative forces, by minds past and present.

I have already explained that we are constantly peopling our own private portion of space by the way we think, and that we are continually being pulled along by the thoughts and desires that we have previously set in motion. Furthermore, the thoughts and desires that we discharge during the course of our lifetime are in turn pulled towards the thoughts and desires set in motion by other people. Collectively they form 'thought strata' in the psychic atmosphere, and they influence the minds of all those with a similar vibration.

Districts, towns and cities, countries and even nations are permeated with the thoughts and desires of all those who live or have lived there. A nation overcome by famine, drought, poverty or war is influenced by the vibratory thought forces which envelop it, rather like clouds hovering in the atmosphere, charging and per-petuating the anguish of those who live there even more, making it virtually impossible for them ever to be free from their never-ending plight. The same principles and laws that operate in the psychic lives of a nation overcome by famine or war also operate in a nation blessed with peace, happiness and wealth.

On a much smaller scale, the thoughts and desires of people, past and present, determine the psychic atmosphere of a building. The thoughts of those who live, or have lived there, psychically impreg-nate the subtle structure of a house, in time creating a living atmospheric personality, which represents the minds of all those who have, and also who still reside within its walls. One often experiences this psychic atmosphere when entering an old building. You may be immediately overwhelmed either by its warmth and friendliness, or perhaps by its coldness and unhappiness.

Although most people have experienced this sort of phenomenon at some time, a psychic person is always open to it and can, on occasion, be deeply affected by it. A psychic person can also be strongly affected by other people's feelings and attitudes towards them. The developing psychic must therefore take measures to safeguard themselves from 'psychic attack', as this can, if allowed to persist, lead to deterioration in health. A 'psychic attack' does not necessarily have to be intentional to have an effect upon the sensitive mind. Hate, jealousy or malice secretly directed towards the psychic can wash over his or her aura like waves of electricity, temporarily altering the polarity of their electromagnetic energy field, eventually causing feelings of depression, being under-the-weather, and possibly complete disorientation.

The effects of such an attack are, however, largely transitory. Should there be no real, rational reason for it – i.e. the victim is innocent – it will eventually be redirected, to return to the sender with a force far greater than that with which it was first despatched. We would do well to remember the ancient precept, 'Curses and blessings come home to roost', that is, like will always attract like, in accordance with the great law of karma.

Psychic work can eventually lower one's general resistance, making one susceptible to all sorts of minor ailments. An undisciplined psychic may be prone to depression, and if of a nervous disposition to begin with they may eventually find themselves more so, if precautionary measures are not taken. A healthy, well-balanced diet should be included in your training programme, along with plenty of fresh air and exercise, and a period in the day for turning off completely and relaxing.

You must learn to respect your psychic abilities, and never abuse them, as many people do. Do not be persuaded to use them as a party piece. Should you persist in abusing, or overusing your abilities, they will certainly cease to be as effective, and will cause you psychological distress at a later date.

Some of the most effective methods of preventing loss of vitality are also some of the most simple. Do not underestimate their effectiveness because of their simplicity.

When one is stressed or anxious, or perhaps recovering from a bout of flu or some other debilitating illness, the breathing becomes shallow and quick and the heartbeat fast, causing more loss of vitality. By relaxing the body as completely as you can, and breathing in a specific, rhythmical way, it is possible to restore the body's vitality, thereby aiding recovery.

• •

Exercise 12

The effects of this exercise will prove beneficial, even for the person with no interest in psychic development, and will help to revitalize the brain in times of stress.

- Sit comfortably by an open window, or better still (weather permitting), in the garden. First, ascertain your normal heartbeat by placing your fingers on your pulse. Sit quietly for a few moments, whilst establishing the rhythm of your heart in your mind.

- The vibratory rhythm of your body must correspond with the frequency of each heartbeat, which is referred to as a pulse unit. Breathing with a specific rhythm controls the flow of energy (prana) into the body, and prevents any unnecessary loss of vitality, which may often occur in the case of stress or illness.

- In this particular exercise we are working to a rhythm of 6/3. When you feel quite calm and comfortable, and have fully established the rhythm of your pulse in your mind, place your hands gently on your lap and close your eyes.

- Breathe in for the count of six pulse units; hold your breath for the count of three; breathe out for the count of six pulse units, and then count three between breaths.

- Repeat the whole process again for about eight or ten minutes.

- For the next part of the exercise clasp your hands in front of you, across your solar plexus. This 'seals the channel', so to speak, and prevents loss of prana.

- Still keeping your eyes closed, breathe in with the same slow and easy rhythm, ensuring that the inhalations and exhalations are evenly spaced. Visualize streams of coral-coloured – or pink – energy passing in through your nostrils, down into your lungs and then into the solar plexus.

- Holding your breath for the count of three pulse units, allow the vibrant energy to circulate around the solar plexus in a clockwise motion, then gradually infusing the energy with the negative colour grey, or even black, expel it forcibly to the count of six pulse units.

- Repeat this exercise a few times until you feel totally revitalized, then sit quietly with your eyes closed, allowing prana to circulate in your body.

- It is quite usual to experience some tingling either on the face and forehead, or in the hands and fingertips. This is one of the ways in which currents of pranic energy manifest, and it confirms that the exercise has been done correctly.

- Once you have familiarized yourself with your own bodily rhythm, it will no longer be necessary to count the pulse units with your breathing. You should eventually allow your mind to drift from the counting, and just be aware of the inflowing and outflowing rhythm of your breathing, allowing you to become almost unconscious of the actual process of breathing.

This exercise is ideal for 'recharging the batteries' after a tiring day at work, or even when you are preparing for a job interview, or going into some other stressful situation. It has the effect of sweeping the aura with prana and infusing the chakra system with vitality, thereby boosting your reserves of psychic energy. This sort of rhythmic breathing has an incredible psychological and physiological effect upon the person by holistically infusing the channels with prana.

Chapter Four

Looking Forward Through Time

I t is perhaps only over the last 17 years or so that science has made any real effort to comprehend the concept of time, to the extent that one notable scientist has had to rethink his theories about time and the possibility of travelling through it.

Time is one of those great mysteries that man has always found difficult to comprehend, although it has always held a great fascination for the writers of science fiction who have exploited the subject to the full, exciting and catching the imagination of millions of readers with stories of time travel and time exploration.

In fact, to enable man to live with time, he has arbitrarily divided it into a past, a present and a future. He restricts himself to the confines of the past and the present, thinking the future to be beyond the range of his vision. He compartmentalizes the events that he has already experienced into the section of his memory labelled 'the past', and at times he apparently has great difficulty in dealing with the present, until that, too, is ready to be placed in the section labelled 'the past'.

Man has little difficulty in recalling the past to the present, but he tends to perceive the future rather like a blind man wandering alone in some strange, mysterious land, almost as though he has an inherent dread of it. In fact, from the moment we are born we are conditioned to believe that we cannot see the future, and that the future is in the lap of the gods.

Space, however, appears to present a far smaller problem to man. This, at least, seems to be more apparent to him, inasmuch as he is able to move more freely in space than he can in time. He can move forward, backward and sideward in space, and now he has learned to move outward and upward, thus conquering the limitations imposed upon his predecessors, by designing and building flying machines and spacecrafts.

It would thus appear that science is now only just beginning to bring into reality the images, impressions and dreams of the science fiction writers of the last 60 years or more. Could it therefore be that the mind is truly the common denominator? Could each one of us be linked to the other, and could all in some way be connected to a universal reservoir, in which the past, the present and the future are experienced as one *eternal NOW*? Is it not a fact that the astronaut makes a mockery of time when he perceives the earth from a great height, with the nights, days and time differences of all the countries in the world visibly manifesting together, all at the same time?

We are most certainly limited, in more ways than one, by our brains and the way in which they have evolved. The rearrangement of a cerebral lobe, and the addition of a fine network of nerves to those which form our consciousness, would no doubt be all that is needed to make the future unfold itself before us, with the self-same clarity and majestic amplitude as that with which the past is displayed upon the horizon of our memories.

Perhaps in the future man will have mastered the art of manipulating time, and travelling through it. If this is true, and the future has already happened, why has no one travelled back to inform us of what they know? Perhaps they have, and perhaps the past to which future man has travelled is not the present that we know and are experiencing at this moment in time.

Perhaps the universe itself is not what it appears to our

ephemeral minds. It is certainly multidimensional by its very nature, with worlds existing within worlds, each rising in a gradually ascending vibratory scale, from those which touch and blend with the highest vibratory dimensions of the physical world, to those which gradually merge with the lowest vibratory dimensions of the great astral world.

Man, it would appear, is used to mentally looking in one direction, and that is to the past. He regards the future as being out of bounds, and is probably afraid of what he might see. The future has always held a great fascination for him – a curious, and at times naïve fascination, that was often exploited by the ancient seers and visionaries whom he would consult for information about his future. Needless to say, not all seers in ancient times were genuine. However, those who were had long since discovered a way of gaining access into that mysterious land of the future, even though some of the strange and weird methods of divination used by them would no doubt be ridiculed or frowned upon today. Some seers, such as the great Nostradamus, imbibed a herbal narcotic to enable them to glimpse the future and to then make their predictions about the things they glimpsed there. However, some seers needed nothing at all to help them to see into the future, and would often appear to stare vacantly into space in order to glean the information they required.

Once your psychic ability has shown signs of manifesting, the art of 'staring' can be perfected with practice, and the ability to perceive the future developed in time.

It is possible that your psychic ability presently manifests as no more than strong intuitive feelings, and that you neither see nor hear anything that could be regarded as a psychic experience. You may also still have a lot of self-doubt regarding the possibility of your being psychic, and you may still discount any strong, extraordinary feelings that you experience, putting them down to intuition.

However, you must understand that intuitive abilities manifest through the same faculties as do psychic abilities, and they are often all that remains in most people of the primitive mechanism of the survival faculty used by our prehistoric forebears.

The devout sceptic denies the existence of psychic abilities, but will readily accept the existence of intuition, simply because it is traditionally accepted by society, while psychic abilities are not. It would be extremely difficult to describe the taste of sugar to someone who has never tasted anything sweet, or to describe colour to a person who has been visually handicapped from birth. It is equally difficult to describe exactly what a psychic vision is like to a person who has never experienced one.

We have all experienced the natural phenomenon of day-dreaming – staring blankly into space as nebulous pictures pass, sometimes nostalgically, across our consciousness. But, while day-dreaming, how many times have pictures or images that you did not recognize float across your mind? You therefore discounted them, putting them down to pure imagination.

The faculty responsible for the psychic ability of clairvoyance manifests in various unexpected ways. The images produced through the process of daydreaming also manifest from that same faculty, and can be developed and cultivated with the use of the same techniques. But what use would there be in developing the ability to daydream, merely to recall pictures of one's past?

Daydream into the Future

I have used the term 'daydreaming' as an example, in order to help you understand exactly how most clairvoyant impressions appear. They can often be quite nebulous, even when the ability has been developed into a fine art. Even when one has undergone extensive training, and possesses an extremely accurate psychic ability, demonstrations of such powers must always be looked upon as purely experimental, because the results are rarely consistent, and cannot therefore be guaranteed. However, practice does make it as perfect as it can be, and helps to bring it more under you conscious control.

. . . .

Exercise 13

- Take a piece of matt-black cardboard, measuring approximately 2ft (60cm) square, and paint a white dot in the very centre.

- Take a piece of white cardboard of the same size, in the centre of which you should paint a black dot.

- Prop up both cards in front of you, facing you and as near to eyelevel as possible. They should be at a distance of approximately 3ft (90cm) from you.

- Spend a few moments relaxing, eyes closed, and making the mind quiet.

- Breathe slowly and deeply, still with your eyes closed, allowing your stomach to rise as you breathe in, and to fall as you breathe out. Continue this for a few minutes.

- Once you are perfectly relaxed, open your eyes and slowly move your gaze to the white dot in the centre of the black card.

- Focus your gaze on this dot, resisting the temptation to blink or to move your eyes away even for a moment, as this will defeat the object of the exercise. Should you find it impossible to gaze without blinking, then blink, but do not move your eyes away from the centre dot, even for a split second.

- When you can gaze no longer, close your eyes and place your hands over them. Wait for a few moments until the after-image appears in your mind's eye.

- Watch the after-image float around your consciousness for a few moments, breathing in and out slowly and deeply, willing the after-image to become brighter and more clearly defined every time you breathe in. Retain the after-image in your mind's eye for a few moments, and then turn your attention to the white card.

- Open your eyes and allow your gaze to focus on the black dot in the centre of the white card. Repeat the staring process.

- As you gaze at the black dot, notice how the previous after-image of the black card appears to be superimposed over the white card. Continue to gaze at the black dot, resisting any distraction you may feel from the previous after-image.

- When you can no longer hold your gaze, slowly close your eyes and watch the new after-image being introduced into your consciousness.

- Continue this exercise for a maximum of 15 to 20 minutes, alternating cards each time you repeat the process.

Practise this exercise at least three times a week, more if possible. This particular scrying technique has the effect of stimulating the image-making faculty, and eventually precipitates the clairvoyant ability.

The person who has no great difficulty in visualizing images and who can create pictures in the mind's eye with ease has a far greater chance of developing the ability of clairvoyance than the person who cannot visualize. The process of clairvoyance involves creative energies and is encouraged by the image-making faculty of the brain. Artists, or any people who work in a creative field, quite often possess potential psychic abilities, and they probably experience these in their work from time to time without even realizing it.

Exercise 14

- This exercise should be practised with a partner in order to obtain the best positive results.

- Use only the black card (*see* Exercise 13). Sit in front of the propped-up black card and ask your partner to sit behind it. Place a cassette recorder beside you to record the whole experiment.

- Tell your partner to mentally project a picture to you through the back of the black card, while you focus your gaze on the white dot. The projected picture can be anything at all, from a simple landscape to a complex geometric shape.

- While gazing at the white dot you should allow your mind to remain passively empty, making no attempt to receive the picture your partner is sending.

- When you can no longer gaze at the dot, close your eyes and place the palms of your hands over them, watching the after-image appear very slowly in your mind's eye. It is approximately at this point that your partner's mental impression should gradually become visible to you.

- At first nothing may happen, but if you persevere with the experiment you will begin to receive faint fragmented impressions. Of course, you may not see anything very clearly at all, and may just be overwhelmed with vague sensations. Whatever you experience, you must voice it immediately, as this often encourages any impressions received to grow stronger and much clearer.

- If at first you are not successful, ask your partner to transmit another picture. In my experience the composition of the picture is not important. It can be anything from a simple image to an extremely complex pattern – it does not matter which. If the exercise is going to work, it will work just as well with an intricate design as with a single, solitary line.

Once you have mastered the technique, and developed a rapport with your partner, a telepathic relationship should become apparent in the results that you obtain. By practising this sort of exercise, you will eventually discover your own technique and way of achieving the desired results.

● ●

Most people who show even the smallest interest in psychic matters often do so because of an experience which they themselves have had at some time or another, and which has left them with the feeling that there is more to be developed. When cornered, even the most ardent cynic will admit that they have had an unusual psychic experience at some time.

The most common experience, and one which most people say they have had, is that of knowing of someone's death long before the news arrives. Or knowing the phone is going to ring before it does, and perhaps even knowing who the caller will be. These kinds of experiences (precognitive experience) transcend the bounds of coincidence, particularly when they happen more than once.

I have often heard it said of psychics that they possess overactive imaginations, or that they are too sensitive. These accusations are correct on both counts. A strong, active imagination appears to be a prerequisite for the development of psychic abilities, and the stronger the abilities the more sensitive the psychic. I would hope that with the help of the exercises in this book you will be able to control your sensitivity, and learn to channel it in a positive way.

Furthermore, in order to develop your psychic abilities further, you must allow your imagination to work for you. To suppress it in any way will merely inhibit any latent psychic tendencies. You must, therefore, give your imagination its freedom, and allow your creative faculties to be active. The following exercise is an example of an experiment in which your imagination can be used. It may prove to you that there is an extremely fine line between what we know as a psychic experience, and what we call imagination.

Exercise 15

- For this experiment you will need to work with your partner again.

- Find an empty box with a lid. A shoebox will suffice.

- Close your eyes and sit quietly.

- Ask your partner to place a small object of their choice inside the box and close the lid. (Obviously, you must not know what object your partner has chosen.)

- Visualize the box surrounded by a very bright white light.

- Imagine yourself breathing the bright white light into your lungs and into your solar plexus.

- Continue to focus all attention on the image of the box in your mind.

- Look upon the box as a conscious entity, full of life, to which you can speak. If it helps you, make it into a sort of cartoon-like character with features, such as eyes, a mouth and legs, etc. Animate the box in your mind, and let it be willing to both listen and talk to you.

- Ask the box to reveal its contents to you. Wait for the answer. No matter how ridiculous the answer seems, repeat it to your partner, who should tell you immediately whether or not you are correct.

- Limit yourself to six attempts at discovering the box's contents. Should you not be successful by then, ask your friend to exchange the article for another, and then repeat the whole process again.

- If you have difficulty in picturing the box as an animated cartoon-like character, focus all your attention on the image of the box in your mind. You must endeavour to make it extremely clear and solid, almost as though you can reach out and touch it.

- Slowly rotate it in your mind, and look at it from all angles, from each side, from the top, from the back, even from the bottom.

- Image yourself picking up the box to ascertain its weight. While mentally holding it in your hands, see yourself lifting the lid and peering inside. You should tell your partner the first thing that comes into your head.

- Should you be correct, repeat the experiment with another article straightaway.

Remember, this is an exercise to help cultivate the image-making faculty, and positive results are not that important. The object of the exercise is to train you to use your imagination, a prerequisite for the cultivation of clairvoyance.

It is important that you do not question how you obtained successful results in this exercise. Do not add doubt by saying it was achieved by guesswork, as how you do it is not important. If you achieve a success rate of six or more out of ten, apparently by guessing, then that is the way it will work for you. Accurate information is often obtained by psychics who appear to 'guess'. Once a psychic ability develops, the way in which it works for you should not be questioned, as long as it is a reliable method that produces positive results.

• •

Precognitive abilities – glimpses of the future – which I touched upon above, are more common than one might imagine. They often display themselves as overwhelming feelings of apprehension, perhaps a strong, intuitive feeling regarding a stranger, or an approaching situation. Sometimes we are 'impressed' to act on impulse, or we perhaps feel pleasurable anticipation about an approaching opportunity, or about a situation that, to everyone else, appears quite depressing.

These strong feelings may only occasionally be experienced, and they often come without any preliminary warning. Nonetheless, they are very real to the person who experiences them, and should therefore be accepted as one of probably many psychic abilities that he or she possesses.

Looking Forward

Even though you may now possess a fairly strong and reliable psychic ability, you may still not yet have developed, or mastered, the art of looking forward into the future. You may have imposed limitations upon yourself by only experimenting with those methods whose results can be immediately confirmed.

Before attempting to develop the skill to look into the future, you must try and understand that by controlling the mind, instead of allowing the mind to control you, you can influence the dynamic forces of the future. You can control circumstances and events before they actually happen, and watch them unfold across your consciousness, as though viewing a television programme which nobody else can see.

This is rather different from precognition, although I do not doubt that the faculty through which precognition manifests is also responsible for the gift of prophesying the future.

In theory, precognition and prophetic vision are the same, but with one small difference. Precognition is mostly involuntary, and the gift of prophecy, although it can happen spontaneously, can very often be controlled.

Before any attempt is made to develop the ability to prophesy the future, you should first have some understanding of the principles underlying the mechanics of awareness. Human awareness manifests at four different levels, and one's conscious-ness has experience at all of these levels at some time or another, often without one even realizing it.

For instance, you may be driving home from work through the rush-hour traffic. Mentally you are going over the day's stressful events, or perhaps you are preoccupied with the arrangements for the coming evening's dinner party. You suddenly become aware that you have parked your car in front of your house, and you have done so with no recollection at all of the journey you have just made.

It would almost seem as though, within us all, there is an 'automatic pilot' which takes over when we are out of control. The same can be said when we are faced with an arduous task for the first time, and one that demands a great deal of concentration. While our attention is focused entirely upon the job at hand we are oblivious to all else around us, and completely unaware of any sound or distraction. However, once the task has been mastered it can be brought under the control of our 'automatic pilot', and, if necessary, be carried out with little or no concentration.

The first and lowest level of human awareness is one that we all experience, all the time. Through this level we gain our knowledge of the world in which we live. The second level of awareness is also shared by everyone, but usually only in times of stress, anxiety, or activation of the survival reflex – that is, when we are under threat of danger.

However, the examples I have given above are in the extreme. In actuality, this second level of awareness is also the aspect of consciousness in which we are capable of achieving extraordinary things. It is subdivided into two aspects: the first takes control of our anxieties and the need to survive, and the second appears to elevate our consciousness into and through the third level of awareness, so bringing about a greater realization of the impulses received from the fourth level of awareness, which is that of spirit.

We are limited by terminology in our definitions of these levels of awareness, so I will refer to them as *physical awareness, instinctive awareness, intellectual awareness* and *spiritual awareness*.

Intellectual awareness represents the thinker in man. It is the level at which he enquires and analyses. It represents the 'I' consciousness, through which man seeks knowledge and expression. Depending on the degree of consciousness he has of the fourth level (that of spiritual awareness), the intellectual level of awareness can be extremely cold, arrogant, self-opinionated and cynical. At its more positive, the intellectual level of awareness brings man ideas and makes him an innovator. Through this level the higher spiritual, or real, self can express its feelings, bringing into man's consciousness spiritual revelations, light and inspiration.

Through the fourth level, spiritual awareness, man experiences divine inspiration and closeness to God in that place of light. Having experienced a level of spiritual awareness, man realizes that words alone will not in any way represent what he has discovered. His tongue appears ineffectual, almost as though some secret command has been given, hushing him to silence.

The spiritual level of awareness does not in any way overpower the third level of intellectual awareness; it simply transcends it, passing down to it the experiences encountered in its own level of consciousness. These are yet again explored at the level of intellectual awareness, whereupon man analyses and reasons about them.

Before attempting to use your psychic powers to prophesy the future, you need first of all to experience the various levels of awareness at which they are acquired, to enable the route of entry to be reliably accessible. In this way results can be successfully achieved each time.

Exercise 16

This exercise has been designed to enable you to experience varying degrees of emotional, mental and spiritual awareness. It often brings out suppressed emotions, by making you aware of old and deeply buried fears, anxieties and sorrows. It is more an exercise in self-awareness than in meditation, and often promotes a greater realization of the soul and its independence of the body. It is a good idea to read through the exercise a few times to ensure that it is firmly fixed in your mind and that you do not have to keep checking it to see what to do next.

- To achieve the desired results, the exercise must be practised with total dedication. Allow it to create for you a sanctuary, or inner sanctum, into which you can retreat when seeking peace and serenity.

- Find a comfortable chair and relax for a few moments with your eyes closed. Make your mind as quiet as you possibly can.

- Breathe slowly and deeply for a few moments, relaxing as you do, and focusing your thoughts totally upon yourself.

- Silently, say to yourself: 'My body is not me. I merely reside in it. I may leave it at any time I wish, but I must return to it when the exercise is concluded.'

- Use this as a sort of mantra, primarily to programme your mind in preparation for the exercise. Repeat it three or four times, fixing it firmly in your mind. Then begin.

- Imagine yourself staring at the worn stone steps of a beautiful old monastery. Look down at the steps and notice the texture and colour of the stone, and the uneven cracks running through them.

- The ornately carved oak doors of the monastery slowly open, and as you look up you see the aged, frail figure of a monk standing on the threshold. Your eyes take in the heavy brown cloth of his habit, and the pale skin of his elderly, wrinkled face. He smiles at you and raises a hand in a welcoming gesture.

- Follow the monk as he turns and walks through the doorway into the monastery. As the doors slowly close behind you they bring a veil of stillness down around you, and you become aware of the quiet, calm atmosphere of the monastery.

- Follow the old man as he makes his way slowly down a shadowy passageway, lit only by flickering lamps strategically positioned on the stone walls either side of you.

- Dark shadows reach across the floor in front of you, and your heart quickens in anticipation as you hasten to keep up with the old monk, whose shuffling footsteps echo off the walls.

- You eventually emerge into a huge, round, brightly lit hall. The high, domed, stained-glass ceiling allows a cascade of colour to pool down upon the marble, mosaic floor, which appears to glisten and sparkle as if it, too, is made of glass.

- As you look around you notice that the walls of the hall appear translucent as they shimmer like mother-of-pearl.

- You notice several monks moving contemplatively around you, chanting to an accompaniment of chimes. For a moment you remain still, listening to the chanting.

- Smiling, your elderly guide gestures towards a doorway on the other side of the hall. You obediently walk across the cool marble floor towards it.

- By the time you reach the door it is already open. Through the doorway you can see a narrow wooden staircase leading upwards.

- Move towards it, and stand for a moment at the foot of the stairs.

- Watch the sunlight stream in through a high window on the landing above you, throwing shards of bright light across the floor and walls.

- In the distance you can still hear the rhythmic chanting of the monks.

- Begin to slowly ascend the stairs, one step at a time, feeling a rush of excitement as you climb higher and higher.

- Follow the staircase as it turns to the left. A few more steps and you find yourself standing alone on the first landing, gazing curiously down the long narrow passageway in front of you.

- There is a sweet fragrance in the air and a sense of peace and wellbeing overwhelms you. You become aware of an extremely strong, familiar feeling of having been there before.

- As you look along the passageway you notice three doors on the left hand side and two doors on the right.

- At the far end of the passage, facing you, there is one door. Pause for a few moments before moving to the door of your choice.

- Before choosing a door it is important to realize that at this level you are given the opportunity to deal with all those negative, self-destructive thoughts and emotions. You are now at the second level, or what I call 'instinctive awareness', and it is important that, upon entering the room of your choice, you either immediately rearrange it to your liking, or simply remove an item of furniture, or anything else you find unpleasant, from the room. Before you leave the room you must feel comfortable with it.

- Now, enter the room of your choice, and close the door gently behind you. Have a good look around. Observe the walls, the windows, the furniture, and the rugs on the floor. Sit down on a chair for a few moments, imbibing the atmosphere.

- Now you must leave. Move towards the door. Pause for a moment to have a last look around the room. Open the door and move into the corridor, closing the door behind you as you leave.

- Before moving away from the room, mentally prepare yourself for the next level – that of 'intellectual awareness'. This is the level at which ideas will come to you. You will feel strongly inspired at this level, and may even decide that you do not wish to go any further. Should this be the case, do not in any way question the apprehension you feel; simply leave, and return to the ground floor, the first level.

- Now continue along the corridor to the staircase at the end. Climb the stairs very slowly, allowing your hand to brush against the cool stone wall. It feels solid and secure beneath your fingers. Once again the feeling of anticipation rushes through you. Within moments you reach the next level.

- At the top of the stairs you move directly into a small study. There are shelves and shelves of books around the walls, and a desk, upon which you notice a writing quill resting in an inkwell.

- There is a blank piece of parchment lying next to the inkwell. A fire is burning brightly in the fireplace, which is surrounded by a beautifully designed mantel. You can feel the heat from the flames as they roar up the chimney.

- Sit in the armchair in front of the fire for a few moments, allowing the peace and serenity of the study to wash over you. At the same time reflect upon your visit to the monastery, and your reason for coming.

- This level is often productive of symbols, ideas and overwhelming feelings. Make your mind completely open to them.

- Rise from the chair and move over to the desk. Take the quill firmly in your hand and scribble on the parchment the first word that comes to mind.

- Have a good look around the room. Feel contemplative, and yet mentally alert, and completely open to the impulses from the next level – that of 'spiritual awareness'.

- Make a mental note of what you have written on the parchment, and move away from the desk.

- Leave the study and walk back towards the head of the staircase. Your eyes search for the way up to the next level, spiritual awareness. There do not appear to be any stairs up to the next level. Stand for a few moments contemplating the way forward.

- You suddenly realize that the only access route to the fourth level is through your own imagination.

- Imagine yourself standing and holding out your arms, whilst staring upwards.

- Imagine an intense white light above you, as if shining through the ceiling.

- Allow the bright light to slowly descend and envelop you, and feel it all around you, interpenetrating every cell of your body.

- You feel totally disorientated and lose all sense of your surroundings.

- Almost at once you feel the bright light gradually fading into nothingness, and you find yourself standing in a beautifully lit sanctuary, in the centre of which there is a comfortable armchair.

- Sit down in the chair and enjoy the peace, the quiet and the solitude.

- Feel totally at peace in the sanctuary, allowing your imagination to create whatever it wishes. Be aware of every aspect of your surroundings, and of the sweet fragrance wafting over you in the stillness.

- Remain there for as long as you wish. It may be that you will lose all sense of time, for time does not exist at the fourth level, where all the answers lie.

- When you are ready to leave, simply allow the quiet sanctuary to slowly fade from your consciousness. Find yourself standing at the top of the stairs, on the third level.

- Move slowly down the stairs, taking in your surroundings as you descend, eventually reaching the second level. Without pausing, continue to move down the stairs to the ground floor and the first level.

- Pass through the small door into the spacious round room with the domed ceiling and the mosaic floor. There the elderly monk greets you. This time, pay particular attention to his aged, lined face. Notice his eyes, which are warm and friendly. Feel secure and safe with him, for next time you must greet him as an old friend.

- Follow the old man across the mosaic floor, this time paying attention to the intricate detail in the design of the patterns on the floor.

- Follow him back along the shadowy passageway until you reach the monastery doors. Open them and move outside into the cool, fresh breeze that gently touches your hair.

- Turn to bid your guide farewell, and mentally ask him if you may return. He nods his answer with a smile, and then closes the door.

- Breathe very slowly and deeply a few times, and dissolve the exercise completely from your mind. Relax for a few moments in your chair until you feel less disorientated.

This has been a psychological exercise in awareness, and it is one that must be used as often as possible in order to obtain the best results. You will find whatever you desire to know of the future at the fourth level. However, it will take time and patience before you achieve the desired results. Once the energies have been created in the exercise, your prophetic intuition will be encouraged to produce glimpses of anything you wish to see.

• •

Once you have developed an affinity with the exercise, and you have come to understand it fully, you can begin to explore its possibilities in a more confident way. Having confidence in the exercise, and allowing yourself to become totally involved with it, is of primary importance. However, the most difficult result to accept and to deal with can often be the sudden rush of feelings, which eventually surface from the bottom of the pool of emotion. Although the exercise appears to be quite simple, you would be wise not to underestimate its benefits.

In the early days, when I used this exercise as an integral part of my own training programme, I noticed that my dreams became more lucid, often producing meaningful prophetic symbols, which helped me immensely with my own life. This changed much later on, once I discovered a positive method of using my dreams as a means of answering the questions I asked of the future. It will all, of course, take time and a lot of patience. But I am quite certain that successful results will be achieved once you have established a relationship with this exciting exercise in awareness. Remember, though, that it is a psychological exercise, and such exercises can be emotionally painful. Should you find that this is the case, then you would be well advised not to abandon it on the grounds that you find the experience far too painful. Once you have passed through the initial stages of the exercise and used it a couple times, you should find it more enjoyable. In the long run the benefits should prove to be incredibly rewarding. Stay with it, and remember: 'The thousand-mile journey begins with a single step.'

Chapter Five

Group and Solo Work

Some people may feel that the support of a group around them can be of great benefit when endeavouring to develop their psychic skills. The encouragement received from a group can be an immense source of strength, as well as a confidence booster, particularly when the positive results you are seeking are not immediately forthcoming.

The one thing that can cause some disappointment, however, when working in a group, is that every one of its members expects total dedication, support and encouragement from the rest of the group – something that is simply not possible. The group must be in total agreement about helping the one whose psychic development is the most advanced, and who, therefore, needs the group's collective energies to be focused totally on them. The envy and jealousy that often arise can create an extremely destructive force, which will work against those aspiring towards the development of psychic powers.

But, in saying this, group activity can work, and can produce some brilliant psychics, particularly when all the members of the group have an affinity with each other, and are therefore able to work together in total harmony.

Although working by yourself does have its advantages, and quite often its rewards, working in a group brings a much greater sense of freedom to your own developing powers, and the combined energies of the group can often bring about some startling results. Working through one's development within a group, as opposed to working alone, calls for a completely different approach, even though most of the methodology used to precipitate psychic abilities is the same.

Results often appear to manifest far sooner with a group approach to development compared with individual work. Perhaps the greatest danger here is that, individually, each member may come to rely far too much on the collective energies of the group, and may, therefore, experience some difficulties when the time arrives for them to work alone. To prevent this from happening it is advisable for each member to be given a working programme, especially designed for him or her to use alone. This enables the developing psychics to be independent, self-sufficient, and able to rely upon their own energies.

I would suggest that each member works through their own programme, by themselves, the same number of times each week (or month) that the group meets. It is better, but by no means essential, to have an even number of members in your group and, if possible, an equal number of men and women, in order to create and maintain a well-balanced flow of energy. A group that works well can create psychic energy very easily. This energy can be used for specific reasons, such as healing, or for affecting telekinetic activity, i.e. causing objects to move without any physical assistance. It can also be created by a group for the purpose of precipitating each individual's chakra system, or, by the use of a specific exercise, such energy can be created and then transferred from one person to the other, producing some extraordinary results.

Exercise 17

Some years ago I designed this exercise for use in a group I was leading. I call the exercise 'The spiralling mantra', for reasons that will become apparent to you later on. It creates such power that everyone is affected, both those in the group and those who remain outside it. The spiralling mantra is very effective in the revitalization of the chakra system, and it also somehow energizes the collective auras of the group, promoting alertness and sharpness of the senses. The spiralling mantra is also extremely effective in the process of *environmental cleansing*, an extremely useful exercise when the energies in a building are uncomfortably unbalanced.

Step One

- Form a circle (using chairs) with, if possible, males and females seated alternately. Should equal numbers of males and females not be present, don't worry; just seat them as best you can.

- Each person's left hand should be turned palm up, and their right hand palm down.

- Touch hands with the person either side of you, until the complete circuit has been created all around the circle.

- With your eyes closed, the group should now spend five or ten minutes breathing rhythmically, slowly and deeply, ensuring that the breathing of everyone in the group is completely synchronized.

- Begin to imagine a pulsating stream of pure white light

passing around the circle, flowing from one person to the next, along the arms and through the hands.

Step Two

- The group should now begin to chant a specific mantra.

- Although most words with symbolic meaning will create energy when chanted rhythmically, the word to be used here is *Ksham*. The 'K' is silent in the word Ksham – and it should, therefore, be chanted as 'Sham'. This is quite a powerful mantra and is used to create and release the inherent forces within Ajna, the brow chakra.

- The group should not chant the mantra exactly in unison, but should slightly stagger each one, leaving one second between each intonation.

- The first person in the group should begin to chant, inhaling deeply before commencing. (The person to begin should be a man to provide a strong deep tone of voice.) He should chant the word 'Ksham' on his exhalation, continuing the sound until all his breath has been fully expelled.

- Approximately one second after the first person has begun chanting, the group member on his left (group member two) should also begin chanting the mantra in exactly the same way, maintaining the sound until all the breath has been fully expelled.

- Approximately one second after group member two begins to chant, the group member on her left should also begin, and so on.

- In this way the chanting will travel clockwise around the

circle, each member chanting the mantra 'Ksham' in turn.

- The voices should be sounded as loudly as possible, ensuring that the hands of everyone in the group are connected through the whole of the chanting process.

- Each participant should continue chanting until all the breath has been fully expelled. They should then wait until the sound has completed the circuit and returned to them.

- Then, inhaling a deep breath, they should repeat the chanting a second after the person on their right has begun.

- The whole process of chanting should be repeated for at least ten minutes – longer if possible – and then, on a given instruction, it should be allowed to gradually fade away.

- When the group has fallen silent each person should remain still, in the same position, with their eyes closed, allowing the energy to circulate from one to the other, around the circle.

The effects of the spiralling mantra are quite spectacular. I have never known it not to be performed successfully. It creates an incredible amount of energy, from which everyone feels some benefit.

The spiralling mantra is not as easy to do as it seems. You will need to read through the instructions a few times, and practise the process a few times before you feel confident.

The main purpose of the spiralling mantra is to create energy within the group. Once created, however, the energy cannot be left, and must be discharged, preferably with a specific mission in mind.

It can be discharged for the purpose of cleansing the atmosphere in a building where there is a great deal of negative energy, such as in the case of paranormal activity. This negative energy could perhaps manifest as some disturbing paranormal phenomenon, such as a poltergeist, or anything that disrupts the equilibrium of the atmosphere. The energy created by the spiralling mantra can be extremely effective in the process of restoring normality to a psychically disrupted home, or even the atmosphere pervading a village.

Once this powerful force has been created within a group it may be channelled into healing, either for a particular group of people or, on a much wider scale, for a nation where there is strife, disease or even war. Discharged over a period of time, the energy can affect changes, restoring the general health and vigour of those to whom it is directed. The transformation is very often subtle, but it can also be quite spontaneous, particularly when the process is repeated regularly.

On a much smaller scale, two or even three people who are in need of healing can be seated in the centre of the circle while the chanting is taking place. During the process of chanting it is important that those seated in the centre keep their eyes closed all through the process. They should not cross their legs, and their hands should remain clasped on their laps in front of them. Those who receive the healing treatment in this way nearly always describe the experience as being just like sitting inside a huge bell. The chanting causes them to lose all sense of weight, and produces a feeling of complete disorientation that is nearly always described as an extremely pleasant experience.

Once the chanting has ceased, a feeling of total calm settles over those who have been treated. If they had previously been experiencing any pain, it usually disappears immediately. The 'patient' is often left feeling quite elated and very emotional. At the conclusion of the chanting there should be a period of stillness and complete silence, allowing the group, and those in the centre of the circle, to imbibe the spiralling force.

The exercise should be concluded with a few deep inhalations and exhalations of breath. The hands may then be withdrawn, thereby breaking the circuit. The group should now raise their arms in the direction of the 'patients' in the centre of the circle. With a final exhalation of breath, the energy must then be discharged into the patients, through the group's outstretched arms.

Of course, you may choose to experiment with the spiralling mantra to discover your own way of working with it. Should your group be a small one, you may find it necessary to modify the exercise in some way, and perhaps even use a different mantra. As long as the group is comfortable with the mantra, and it is one you are all familiar with, you should find it just as effective.

Remember, use the spiralling mantra with respect and look upon it as a psychological exercise, as well as a spiritual one. Do not underestimate its effectiveness, for it is an extremely powerful exercise, and one that holds great appeal for those who prefer the more ritualistic approach to healing. The spiralling mantra can be used as an integral part of a healing programme. Although this book is not specifically concerned with healing, the spiralling mantra is an effective way of discharging surplus energy through the process of healing.

Being too focused upon the development of one's psychic skills can cause an unhealthy buildup of psychic energy in one's personal atmosphere. The spiralling mantra is an ideal way of discharging such energy in a positive way, and will also help to 'ground' the aspiring psychic.

You may also like to experiment with the following method, which is usually called *battery healing*, primarily because of the way in which the healing force is created.

• •

Exercise 18

This method can be used with as few as four people to create the healing battery. All you need is the group, and one other person designated to receive healing.

- Seat the 'patient' comfortably, eyes closed, hands resting lightly on their lap. They should be as relaxed as possible; if necessary, talk them through the relaxation process.

- When the patient is calm and relaxed, the rest of the group should move their chairs into a semi-circle in front of him or her, close enough to hold hands with the patient and with each other.

- Using the same process as with the spiralling mantra (Exercise 17), the group member on the patient's right should place his or her left hand, palm down, in the patient's hand, and then place the right hand, palm up, in the hand of the person on their right.

- Continue in the same way around the semi-circle, until the final person places the right hand, palm down, in the patient's left hand, thus making the 'battery' complete.

- At the very moment the circuit is completed, there should be an incredible surge of power through it; nothing, except participation in the actual experience of the exercise, will suffice to describe the feeling.

- The whole group should attune their thoughts to the patient, keeping their breathing in phase with each other, the inhalations and exhalations as nearly in unison as possible.

- This rhythmic breathing should continue for the entire duration of the healing process, and only be allowed to cease when all hands have been released and the circuit broken.

- Incidentally, this method of healing should not be confused with what is termed 'spiritual healing'. The technique of battery healing is of a purely psychic nature, and is produced as a result of the combined energies of the group being channelled into the patient.

- This form of healing is extremely effective in the case of inflammatory diseases, where there is much pain, and also in the treatment of nervous disorders. It is not to be considered as a curative treatment, but used more to restore the body's vitality, encouraging the self-healing process to take place.

Again, as with the spiralling mantra, you may like to experiment with this method, and perhaps use it in a different way. Although the number of people taking part is of little importance, in my experience the more people involved in forming the battery, the better and more powerful the results.

• •

Exercise 19

You may like to try the following experiment with your group. It is called 'the seagull'. This is an experiment in thought transference, and demonstrates just how effective projecting one's thoughts can be.

- First, ask the most psychically inclined of the group to sit at the front, with their back to the others. He or she should sit in a relaxed position, with their eyes closed, endeavouring to attune their thoughts to everyone in the room.

- Hand out to each of the group (but not to the person at the front) small, folded pieces of paper, upon which you have written a word. Tell the members of the group that every word is different, and that they must not allow anyone else to see what their particular word is. Explain to them that they are going to transmit these words to the person at the front, and that part of the experiment's success depends on this secrecy. In fact, every piece of paper will contain the same word, i.e. *SEAGULL*. However, this will only be known to you.

- When everyone is seated, relaxed and ready to begin, ask the group to close their eyes, and to sit for a few moments focused on their word, establishing it clearly in the mind. Tell them that they must now imagine a thin beam of golden light, passing from their forehead to the back of the head of the person seated at the front. Once it is established sufficiently so that they can see this beam of light very clearly in the mind, and they have become totally aware of the force behind it, they should then allow the beam to gradually fade.

- Now the group members can begin to transmit their word, either as a picture that they have created in their mind or simply as the word is written. The group member sitting at the front must allow their mind to remain passive, and yet they should be aware of any thoughts, feelings or impressions that they may experience, calling these out loudly to the group. Should anyone hear their word thus given, they should respond immediately. It is a good idea for the experiment supervisor to make a note of everything that is called out by the person to whom the words are being directed. It can take time for the group to develop a rapport amongst themselves, and most of the things called out initially may be only loosely connected to the 'word'. For example, a picture of a cloud might be received. These may have been transmitted by one of the group along with the picture of a seagull. The sun shining on the horizon may also be received but, again, the seagull may not. The person who is projecting the word often projects the whole scene which they have created around it. So, until the one receiving the pictures has developed the ability to notice detail, only fragments of the whole picture will be received.

• Spectacular results can occur quite spontaneously in this experiment, and would therefore demonstrate the remarkable telepathic abilities possessed by both those transmitting and by the one who is receiving. This method is in no way a test of the psychic abilities of those taking part. It is more an exercise in telepathy and the development of thought transference. Of course, once those participating in the experiment realize that the same word has been given to everyone, it cannot be practised with the same group again. From then on different words can be given to the group, although even then the exercise will not quite work in the same way, and will therefore need to be modified accordingly.

The seagull exercise can prove to be a powerful aid to the training and development of the powers of the mind, and it clearly demonstrates, to all who witness it, just what great potential lies within us all. The experiment demonstrates just how effective our collective forces can be, when focused on one target. In fact, when endeavouring to cultivate your psychic powers you must not underestimate your own abilities, or the things you have yet to achieve. There is, in fact, no such word as impossible where the sciences of the mind are concerned, and it is only by continuous experimentation that you will come to develop and discover the real psychic you.

The image-making faculty of the brain processes the information received from the external world into ideas of forms and colours, after which it is assimilated by the mechanism of the mind, where our consciousness immediately places the data it receives into some semblance of order.

Working with different coloured shapes helps to cultivate the image-making faculty and encourages the development of our mental powers. The conditioning to which we have been subjected throughout our lives limits our perception and range of awareness, preventing us from looking, listening and feeling beyond the range of our five normal senses.

When we look at an object we normally see the front of the object alone, and never the whole, which is of course both the front and the back. In fact, we impose limitations upon our perception of things simply by believing that we are unable to actually 'see' through and beyond matter. We can only see that to which our eyes respond. But, the response of our eyes is extremely limited, and we generally accept these limitations. So, looking at it in this way, we can see how restricted our perception of the world really is.

However, our mind does not have the same limitations of awareness as, for example, our eyes. What our eyes are unable to perceive, our mind certainly can. By training the mind in a specific way, we may develop the ability to direct the consciousness beyond any boundaries. The ability to almost 'look through' solid objects is not as crazy as it may sound, because the cultivation of the mind to penetrate matter is in fact an integral part of being psychic.

Again, I would say that when endeavouring to develop such powers, the imagination must be allowed total freedom. Allowing yourself to 'let go' completely is of paramount importance, and yet another prerequisite in the cultivation of psychic skills. Imposing limitations upon yourself merely restricts your psychic development in more ways than one, and so you really do have to 'believe' that you are capable of cultivating such incredible powers.

Exercise 20

For this exercise you will need a generous quantity of small envelopes, and as many different coloured shapes as possible. They can be made from card or even simple coloured paper. Use squares, circles, stars, oblongs, ovals, triangles, and any other shapes you can think of.

- First of all, place one shape in each envelope and mix all the envelopes together in a box or bag.

- Now, distribute the envelopes among the members of the group.

- Divide the group into pairs.

- As one partner holds up each envelope in turn, the other should endeavour to determine which shape and colour is inside, without actually touching the envelope. Keep a record of your success.

- The technique used in this particular exercise is quite simple, but it takes time and effort to develop. Instead of just staring at the envelope, you should actually gaze 'through' it, almost like staring into space, as though you are daydreaming. In fact, look right through the envelope as though it is not there. Ignore it completely. If you can resist the temptation to blink, all the better; if not, simply hold your gaze for as long as possible before blinking, and then slowly close your eyes.

- Although the after-image of the envelope itself will eventually appear in your mind's eye, other more nebulous images should also be seen. These, however, will be very fleeting, and will appear to come and go as quickly as the blink of an eye. It is important to respond immediately to the first image you see, and not to analyse what you think you may have seen.

- The colour is usually the first thing to appear, and is very often much clearer than the shape. The two may not appear together, so the shape may appear colourless. This is why you must train your mind to watch very carefully. It is simply a case of practising and knowing exactly what to look for, because the images and impressions you receive may not be in any particular order.

- Do not be put off by the simplicity of this exercise nor, for that matter, by your personal views and opinions. In other words, try to think beyond all that you can see, beyond all that you can hear, and beyond all that you can feel. Try not to allow yourself to become disheartened or discouraged by the lack of immediate successful results.

Exercise 21

This exercise has many possibilities, and you certainly do not have to restrict yourself to coloured shapes.

- Ask your partner to stand behind a screen, or even to move into an adjacent room, and to hold an object (unknown to you) in their hands.

- Now, using the same process as in Exercise 20, try to gaze 'through' the wall, ignoring it completely, and resisting the temptation to blink. The most difficult part of this exercise is trying to ignore whatever obstructs your vision. However, once you have learned to 'block out', so to speak, you will find that it is just as easy to ignore a wall as it is an envelope in order to see whatever is obscured from your field of vision.

- Continue the gazing process for as long as possible, and then close your eyes to receive the imagery. Remember: you are not looking with your eyes – you are using the image-making faculty of your brain, a sort of primitive 'homing' device which you have long since forgotten how to use, to obtain the information.

It is also important to understand that you are not simply using the exercise to obtain information telepathically, but to actually 'see' the object with your mind's eye. This is, admittedly, a little more difficult, but once the technique has been mastered, looking through solid objects, such as walls, will appear just as easy as telepathically receiving information from another mind, without using the intermediary of the senses.

The development of your psychic faculties also amplifies information received via the five physical senses, whose range is somehow increased as a result. Although short-sightedness will not improve with the cultivation of your psychic abilities, your other four senses will certainly compensate for any impairment of your vision.

Considering this sort of sensory amplification, one must expect to be oversensitive at times and prone to mood swings, at least until your development is fully established, and your nervous system adjusts and settles down.

Chapter Six

Mediumship and Talking With the Dead

Before we explore the endless possibilities of the wonderful gift of mediumship, we must first of all get our definitions right.

To begin with, not all mediums are clairvoyant, and not all clairvoyants are mediums. A medium is someone who is able to receive information from the discarnate side of life, either by seeing the so-called 'dead', hearing them or merely sensing them.

The term *clairvoyant* is applied to anyone who has the ability to actually see things that nobody else can, such as situations and events in the future or the past. This sort of information is gleaned through a variety of methods of divination, ranging from tasseomancy (teacup reading) to crystal gazing and cartomancy (reading the cards).

A clairvoyant who possesses the ability to actually see those whom we know to be dead also possesses mediumistic abilities. Although some clairvoyants are able to see discarnate personalities, the absence of other psychic abilities simply makes the information they are able to receive from discarnates very limited.

Although the word 'clairvoyant' is the one with which most people are familiar (it literally means 'clear seeing'), other mediumistic skills include *clairaudience* (clear hearing) and *clairsentience* (clear sensing). It may come as a surprise to learn that, simply by 'sensing' a spirit presence, a medium is quite able to describe everything about the person, from the colour of their eyes and hair to their height and the cause of their death. The gift of clairsentience can be so uncannily accurate that, to onlookers, it often appears as though the medium is actually seeing, hearing and holding a conversation with the spirit of the dead person. However, this is certainly not the case.

The gift of clairaudience or the ability to hear the voices of the so-called dead, contrary to popular belief, is quite rare. However, many clairsentient mediums mistakenly believe that they are receiving their information clairaudiently, simply because their gift of clairsentience can be so clear that it sometimes seems as if a voice is speaking to them.

Although clairaudience involves the auditory faculties controlling the sense of hearing, the spirit voices are not always that clear, and they can manifest in different ways. Sometimes a spirit voice can appear as a muffled sound, almost as though someone is speaking to you from an adjacent room. At other times it resembles a clear voice, audible at your side. Sometimes, however, clairaudient voices appear as no more than extraneous thoughts, passing quickly through the consciousness.

One of the most common misconceptions concerning mediumship is that the medium has the power to call discarnate spirits back and to command communication with them. No matter how well known, or how powerful the medium happens to be, it is simply not possible to command spirit communication. A medium acts as an intermediary between two worlds, a sort of telephone exchange, or even a radio which has to be 'tuned in' to the correct wavelength. If the spirit world decides not to communicate for any reason there is nothing that can be done. For this reason alone, mediumistic communications must always be considered as purely experimental, because the results cannot in any way be guaranteed and it simply does NOT always work. The other thing that should be reiterated at this point is that seeing so-called 'dead' people is far from normal, regardless of what you may believe. Mediumistically inclined people generally tend to be psychologically and emotionally different from those who do not have any such tendencies. Because of the incredible stress on a medium's nervous system, he or she very frequently suffers from incredible mood swings. However, this does not have to be the case. These mood swings are usually brought about simply because of lack of training and the medium invariably lacks discipline and needs to be grounded. My holistic approach to development encourages grounding and helps to promote serenity and focus. Although the majority of mediums have, at some time or another, sat in a so-called development circle, more often than not under the supervision and watchful eye of a qualified medium, in my experience this can sometimes be a hindrance and interfere with the development of mediumistic abilities.

How it all Works

The human organism is an electromagnetic unit of incredible power, assimilating and releasing energy, and is contained within its own spectrum of light and colour. This magnetic field, the aura, interpenetrates the physical body and also reaches out to integrate with other energies. In order to maintain perfect balance in the human organism, such power needs to be controlled, modulated, divided and evenly distributed throughout the body. This is the role of the chakras, which are like small electrical transformers, controlling the inflowing energy and then distributing it to the major organs of the physical body. As stated in Chapter Two there are in fact hundreds of minor chakras situated throughout the subtle anatomy, although there are seven major chakras that are considered primary and these are to be found across the surface of the etheric body in the spinal column, beginning at the base of the spine and finishing at the crown of the head. Each of these chakras

performs a particular function and is responsible for the manifestation of consciousness at its corresponding level.

Up until the age of about seven a child's aura is completely
untainted and only begins to change when adults begin the process
of training and chastising. Although a child is chastised to some
degree long before this age, psychological programming only really
takes place when the chakra system is fully formed. Some children
show obvious signs of mediumistic abilities from a very early age,
and although the majority grow out of it, a very small minority do
not. Children with a propensity towards paranormal abilities on
the whole tend to be quiet and withdrawn and seem to spend a lot
of time daydreaming. Staring into space is quite common for the
psychically inclined child, who very often appears to be lost in his
or her own little world. Although all children daydream, the child
who possesses even a rudimentary form of psychic ability tends to
take every available opportunity to do so. Although this book is not
specifically about psychic children, I think it is important to
highlight the way in which psychic and mediumistic skills evolve
from the early years of childhood, up into adult life.

In saying this, one does not have to be psychic as a child in order
for psychic skills to manifest in one's adult life. On the contrary, there
are innumerable reasons why psychic or mediumistic skills suddenly
appear, one of which may be emotional or psychological trauma.
Illness or even an accident, in which the head has sustained some
injury, may precipitate psychic abilities. And although the reason for
this is not known, some research has shown that changes in the
general condition of the brain are nearly always apparent with the
psychically inclined person. In fact, seeing so-called 'dead' people is
not normal, regardless of what the majority thinks. Abnormalities
are apparent in the brain of a mediumistically inclined person,
and although these abnormalities are very subtle, they do cause the
person to be oversensitive and prone to bouts of depression.

Research carried out in Moscow University in the early part of the 20th century caused one neurological scientist to compromise his professional integrity. His interest in so-called paranormal experiences attracted a great deal of concern from his peers and very nearly caused him to lose his position. Professor Ivan Tutinsky's seven-year paper on the subject led him to conclude that the pineal gland – a walnut-shaped gland deep within the brain – was in fact responsible for paranormal experiences. The professor's conclusions were finally reached when he discovered that the pineal gland of a child was much larger than that of an adult, and much more developed in a female than in a male. This, he wrote, was the very reason why children have so many paranormal experiences, and why women are far more sensitive than men. Although he was ridiculed by his peers, Tutinsky's seven-year research caused him to be converted from the atheist he was, to becoming interested in the whole metaphysical area.

As a musician I could teach a class of 20 students the basic rudiments of the guitar, although only perhaps 2 or 3 would have sufficient aptitude for the instrument to play the guitar to professional standards. It would be the same process with mediumistic skills, with an inherent ability within a small minority. Although psychic abilities can usually be nurtured in almost anyone, to some greater or lesser degree that is, in my opinion mediums are born and not made, and what frequently purports to be mediumship is very often no more than a psychic or intuitive skill. Although psychic skills can appear very impressive, the practitioner is very often self-deluded into thinking that what they have is a mediumistic ability. This simply gives the wrong impression to those who are seriously investigating mediumistic abilities, and is probably one of the primary reasons why mediumistic skills are frequently ridiculed by sceptics. Nonetheless, regardless of how the whole concept of mediumship and psychic skills is viewed by professional sceptics, the interest in the subject has grown immensely over the last ten years.

Developing Mediumistic Skills

Before we move any further I do have to quote a cliché and say, 'mediums are born and most certainly not made'. Whilst everyone possesses psychic abilities potentially, only a small minority truly possess inherent mediumistic skills. Regardless of what you have been told, mediumistic abilities cannot be developed if the potential is not already present. Although a crude analogy, this would be like putting petrol in a diesel-powered vehicle and expecting the engine to run. Nevertheless, the same techniques that are used for the development of psychic skills may be used in the cultivation of mediumistic skills.

• •

Exercise 22

If you are endeavouring to develop your latent powers with a group of like-minded people, arrange for each of them to bring along a friend and seat them in rows in front of you. Ensure that you know nothing about their backgrounds, and that before the experiment begins you have no contact with anyone but the person you have elected to help you. Each person there should be willing to participate in your spontaneous psychic demonstration and should respond to anything that relates to them simply by putting up his or her hand. As previously mentioned, prior to the demonstration, you should arrange for a selected member of the group to act as the intermediary and to tell you whether or not your 'message' has been accepted. In this way it will not be possible for you to make a psychological assessment by reading body language, facial expressions or the sound of the person's voice.

- In order to eliminate the possibility of giving information already known to you, ask someone to blindfold you before you begin.

- At first, do not expect to hear or see anything, but simply use all your senses to 'home in' to your audience. In fact, activate your natural radar system (the aura) by mentally scanning your audience, at the same time watching the little screen of your mind for any images, feelings or extraneous thoughts that may flash through your conscious- ness. At this point you should not worry too much about the content of the information, but as soon as something 'strikes' you, so to speak, relay it immediately to your audience. Your intermediary will tell when the information has been accepted and prompt you to continue.

- Once a connection has been made with one of your audience you should endeavour to maintain that connection with the same person. However, parts of the information may not be accepted by the same person and someone else may respond to it. Your intermediary should tell you when this happens, and then it may be necessary for you to work with two separate recipients.

- Give as much information as you can and try to be as detailed as possible. Should people's names (first and second), places, house numbers and street names pop into your head, relay them immediately. In the initial stages of your demonstration try not to hesitate or analyse the information. Always say what you are feeling, almost without thinking. At the beginning of your development this is the way in which information is processed by the brain. Until you become more confident and adept at working with people you should not question or doubt any of the information you receive. Don't be embarrassed or self-conscious; after all, your audience will understand.

• In the final part of your demonstration you should remove your blindfold and, with the guidance of the person helping you, you should return to the recipients of your messages to see if you can elaborate on the information you gave to them previously. Now that you can actually see the person you should find yourself in receipt of even more detailed information. I'm not suggesting for one moment that a mediumistic skill is suddenly going to develop simply by using this exercise. As with all mental skills, your ability has to be carefully honed with patience and determination. What I am saying is that if the potential is there, the use of certain exercises and methods, such as the ones shown in this book, can safely hasten the process, with little or no need to sit in a so-called 'development circle' for many years.

Exercise 23

For this experiment it may be better to invite a new group of people to work with. The audience should be seated as before, in rows in front of you. This time, though, you are going to play a little game. In fact, this training exercise has two aims:

1 To *develop a mediumistic style and presentation.*

2 To *encourage clairvoyant ability.*

First, introduce yourself to the audience. It should be made clear to everybody that although *you* will be playing a role, those who receive a message will not, and should therefore respond to the information with honesty.

- You will be playing the part of a medium, as though acting out a role in a play.

- Select someone from the group at random and proceed to give that person a 'message', as though the information is being received from someone who is dead. You must of course use your imagination to describe the features and physical stature of the 'dead' person whom you have created in your mind. Without pausing to think about what you are saying you should continue to relate names and personal details, and to say anything and everything that comes into your mind.

- The 'making it up as you go along' approach is all part of the exercise, and it is only at the conclusion of the demonstration that the accuracy of the 'message' will become a reality, when it becomes clear to you just how much of the information is correct and has been confirmed.

- Although both you and the audience may feel as though the whole thing is just a charade, the use of the image-making faculty in this particular way somehow creates a subliminal bridge between the mind of the medium and the spirit world. It is across this bridge that 'connections' are spontaneously made, and during your attempt to create a sort of make-believe demonstration of mediumship, a genuine link with the spirit world filters into your consciousness. Remember, although you may have been 'pretending' or making it up as you went along, the audience was not! I am not suggesting that every bit of information which is given in this way comes from a genuine source. However, I have seen it work successfully so many times that probably 80 per cent or more of the information given during such a demonstration of so-called 'spontaneous mediumship' will accurately be placed.

. . . .

Although the exercise resembles a party game, it is certainly one which can prove invaluable to an aspiring medium, and it is of course most effective in the precipitation of the clairvoyant skill. Remember, a medium can only be judged by the amount of accurate information he or she gives, and so at this point in the process of the development of a mediumistic skill, as long as the information is accepted, how it is received is not that important. Parapsychologists would condemn this explanation and describe the whole process as 'cold reading'. Apart from everything else, this exercise is ideal for cultivating style and technique.

I have already said elsewhere that the gift of clairaudience is quite rare, even though many mediums mistakenly believe that they possess it. It is one of those psychic skills which have to be potentially present before it can be fully developed. Although this is so with all psychic skills to some greater or lesser degree, the cultivation of clairaudience will not be encouraged unless the individual has had some experience of it at some time in his or her life, and such experience usually takes place during childhood. However, should you believe that you possess clairaudient abilities, but your experiences have been quite spasmodic and therefore not under your control, this ability can be refined, thus making the auditory experience more 'amplified' using the following techniques.

It must be said at this point, because of the nature of clairaudience (hearing supersensual sounds, such as disembodied voices), should you have a history of psychological illness, methods to cultivate this ability should be avoided.

Clairaudience has, more often than not, been present from childhood, and the chakra responsible for its manifestation also controls the vibratory impulses that are produced in the small space of the eardrum, causing that sense of 'hearing'. Thus, by preventing the vibratory manifestations of sound from reaching our sense of hearing, we can cause a quickening in the throat chakra in order to encourage its further activation.

. . . .

Exercise 24

After a period of meditation and rhythmic breathing, sit quietly for a further five or ten minutes. Then, if possible, go out into your garden or local park, or sit in front of an open window.

• Close your eyes and count exactly how many different sounds you can hear, such as birds singing, the rustle of leaves, the involuntary cracking of branches, the wind brushing the grass, and any other sounds your senses can pick up. It takes time before you will be able to eliminate the sound of your heart and breathing. Be patient.

• Listen to the sounds beyond the immediate, such as traffic, dogs barking, children playing, an aeroplane overhead, and so on. Be totally aware of your surroundings and beyond, and for a few moments endeavour to become totally attuned to nature. While attuning your thoughts and becoming relaxed, you will probably be able to pick out faraway sounds that are almost inaudible to the physical ear.

- Spend about half an hour on this part of the exercise. Then, still with your eyes closed, plug your ears so as not to permit even the slightest sound to pass into the eardrum. It will probably take a few minutes to adjust to the sudden deafness and the effect can be disorientating. However, something will seem to 'come alive' inside you – at least, that is the best way I can describe the sensation.

- At this point you should try to become totally aware of the vastness of the space around you. The aim here is not to hear specific sounds, but more to develop an inner aware-ness, which will only be achieved when all other distractions have been excluded. It takes time to expand one's aware-ness in this way, but I have never known it to fail.

It may be that at the beginning of the exercise you will hear nothing at all. However, with a serious, determined approach to your psychic development, and with regular practice over a period of time, this exercise should gradually produce positive results. As with most skills, it is important to practise regularly, and although it may be neither practical nor realistic to do so every day, you really should try to find time to work at it at least three times a week in order to get a proper feeling for it.

Once the chakras have settled down to the fact that the senses are being withdrawn, as in the case of hearing, there is usually a sudden quickening of energy in the throat and brow area to compensate for the withdrawal.

Remember: this exercise will only aid the development of the gift of clairaudience if it is already potentially present. In these cases it will help the aspirant to bring it more under their conscious control. The exercise can, however, help to precipitate a much deeper awareness of the senses, attuning them more acutely to the more sublime aspects of the universe.

• •

As with all mediumistic abilities, clairaudience is a gift of the spirit, and should therefore be treated as such. As it develops it should be encouraged, and this can be achieved by laying strong foundations of knowledge and spiritual awareness. Once the great door of the faculties has been opened to the world of the discarnate, those who approach you may not always be of the kind that you would choose to call. The vagabonds, the rogues, the villains and the debauched of this world become themselves, and more so, in the next world, and will still have a need to gratify their low passions and desires.

Discipline and caution make a wise man strong, and where psychic development is concerned you are only as strong as your weakest attribute. It is certainly not the angelic forces alone who seek to help you in your spiritual endeavours, but as you become a beacon of light, as all mediums must be, those vagabonds of the lower astral world, whose sole intention is to prevent such light from manifesting in this world, will be attracted to you also. A medium's path is certainly not an easy one, and may even be a path of pain and emotional turbulence. For your own protection it is important to cultivate the habit of thinking higher and more spiritual thoughts.

There are other skills which come under the umbrella of mental mediumship, and which can also be developed. These are as follows:

Psychic Art

Psychic art is the ability to sketch a portrait of a 'dead' person whose presence has either been intuitively felt, or whose form has been 'seen' by the artist. Should you be in the slightest way artistic, you may consider combining your psychic abilities with your artistic skills, and using them in this way.

Psychic art is a very visual way of working, and it can be compelling when endeavouring to offer proof of someone's continued existence after death. This is, after all, the primary object of mediumship, proving the continuity of the soul beyond death. The same process we used previously with the spontaneous mediumship experiment may also be used to encourage the development of psychic art.

Most of the psychic artists I have known claim to have no clairvoyant skills, and therefore 'see' nothing at all. One can thus only assume that their ability to sketch an accurate portrait of a so-called 'dead' person is done purely through intuitive means. Demonstrating skills as an artist in the spontaneous mediumship experiment will produce the same if not better results, simply because it is more visual.

• •

Exercise 25

The aspiring psychic artist should sit or stand in front of the audience, sketch pad and pencil at the ready. Once again, randomly select a member of the audience.

- The psychic artist can accurately demonstrate his or her ability by simply allowing the pencil to intuitively create the first image (of a person) that comes into their mind. It is important to add a little verbal information as the sketch is being created, perhaps just to describe the

person who is being drawn and to make the
demonstration more interesting.

- Remember, any psychic skill is helped greatly by the
images processed by the image-making faculty, and so it
is vitally important that, whilst the drawing is being
created, the artist actually sees the face of the person
they are sketching in their mind. In other words, the
psychic artist must allow his or her 'imagination' to take
over to create a clear impression in the mind's eye.

Although it is much better if you are artistically inclined to begin
with, it is not of paramount importance. I have known at least
three psychic artists who could not draw at all until they were
using their psychic artistry.

These experiments make the sometimes boring aspects of
psychic development a little more interesting. However, they are
also of prime importance in helping to encourage in the aspiring
medium a more professional presentation and interesting style of
working.

Spirit Writing

Frequently termed 'automatic writing', this is the ability to receive
written messages from disembodied sources, which are always
outside the conscious control of the writer. In fact, the writings are
involuntary, and can sometimes be written when the medium's
mind is occupied elsewhere. The writings usually appear in a script
quite different to that of the writer's normal hand, and are produced
very quickly with no breaks between the words, which nearly always
move from one passage to another with no punctuation.

This writing phenomenon is quite different from the so-called 'inspirational writing' mentioned in the following example.

Once even a rudimentary form of mediumship has been cultivated, it is possible to produce spirit or automatic writing.

Exercise 26

- When endeavouring to develop the ability to demonstrate this sort of phenomenon, it is important to sit at the same time every day or night, and at a time when you are certain you will not be disturbed.

- Before you begin, express your desire to receive written communication from the spirit world. Although this may require a few attempts, it does establish a link with your disembodied communicators.

- Simply sit quietly with a pencil held gently on a blank piece of paper.

- It is important to keep the mind quiet and your thoughts on something other than writing, as this merely defeats the object of the exercise.

To ensure that you do not consciously interfere with the process it is sometimes a good idea to read a book.

If no results are produced after a couple of weeks, then turn your thoughts to inspirational writing for a while, as illustrated in the following example.

Inspirational Writing

Lord Byron once said:

> *Poetry is a distinct faculty; it won't come when called –*
> *you may as well whistle for the wind.*

I am quite sure he was referring to the actual inspiration of poetry. These words should be borne in mind when endeavouring to cultivate the ability to receive inspirational writings, as the whole process takes time to develop.

This is very often confused by many spiritualists as automatic writing, but is completely different. Although not generally thought of as mediumship, in the psychic context it is very much so, and certainly a phenomenon that should not be disregarded.

With this form of writing the writer feels inspired by discarnate minds, who very often appear to use the mind of the writer to express their own philosophical thoughts, views and ideas. During the writing process the medium is totally conscious of what is being written, unlike the automatic writer who is not.

Most, if not all, poets, writers, musicians and even artists have claimed at some time to have been inspired by some supernatural force. Some have even said that without experiencing this force they find it useless to even attempt to write or create anything. This is exactly what Lord Byron was talking about. John Lennon once said that sometimes when he was composing a new song it felt as though the top of his head had opened up to allow a powerful force to flow into his brain.

I have known writing mediums to describe that feeling which overwhelms them when they are inspired to write something, as being akin to some immense power flooding their very being. For me, inspiration causes a quickening of all my senses. I feel totally preoccupied with the theme of what I am writing, so much so that my heart beats fast and my senses become totally oblivious to anyone or anything around me. When I have finished writing it often seems as though some force has lifted from me, leaving me with a strange sense of emotion.

Inspirational writing is not, as I have already said, to be confused with automatic writing, which is completely involuntary. The only feature which inspirational writing and automatic writing have in common is that the writings which are produced most certainly originate from a metaphysical source, over which no control can in any way be exercised.

I rarely have the least idea what I am going to write about before I sit down at my desk. But then I am suddenly overwhelmed with specific feelings which I can usually relate to certain disembodied personalities whom I have come to know, and with whom I have developed a strong relationship over the years. These feelings often mean that a specific theme will be followed in the writings. With this sort of inspirational writing it is usually the intention of the writer to 'link up', so to speak, with some disembodied force, such as a certain spirit guide with whom there is a special affinity. The writing produced is usually outside the knowledge of the writer, and may be in the style of a certain historical period. It usually leaves no doubt in the mind of the writer that it has come from another mind.

It is a common misconception that inspirational writing is easy to produce. It takes some time and a lot of patience to fully develop the subtle process, but when it has successfully been achieved a whole new world opens to the medium. Quite often to begin with, nothing very spectacular happens. With inspirational writing one is inclined to sit there searching the mind for appropriate thoughts to put down, but these often drop into the consciousness without the control of the writer, and may even flood the mind with images, feelings and ideas.

Automatic writing also requires a totally quiet mind, with the attention of the writer directed away from the pen and paper.

. . . .

Exercise 27

- Once you feel an affinity with a certain *spirit helper*, perhaps someone who you know will 'inspire' you with words of philosophical enlightenment, simply sit quietly with a pen and paper.

- Remove all distractions from the room, and ensure that you have at least an hour at your disposal.

- At first it is a good idea to close your eyes for a few moments, primarily to attune your thoughts.

- Allow thoughts and ideas to pass through your mind, and even experiment by writing these down.

- You may at first just produce short, almost meaningless sentences. However, in time these will increase in size and become more meaningful.

As I have previously said, it is better to 'sit' at the same time every evening, and you must be punctual each time you sit. As the concept of time in the spirit world is completely different to that which we know in this world, there being no alternating periods of night or day, it will benefit your 'spirit inspirers' who will be guided by your punctuality. This will also reassure them that you are both serious and dedicated.

. . . .

Using the same process of inspiration one can also find an answer to a specific problem, regardless of what that problem is.

Chapter Seven

Channelling the Powers of the Mind

Most people live out their lives from day to day, completely unaware of the powers that lie within them. A working person often experiences the day's routine almost mechanically, having gone through the same things day in, day out, for years. Regardless of being more or less content or completely dissatisfied with their lives, the majority of people are ignorant of the fact that there are such powers within their minds which, if channelled and released, could transform both themselves and their lives completely.

The poor man only dreams of being wealthy, thinking that riches are far beyond his reach. The weak and sickly person wishes for good health and strength, and the unhappy person hopes and prays for happiness, sometimes never believing that they will ever really be happy. The majority of people live lives of hopes, wishes and dreams, without possessing the knowledge that they could be in control of an inner power that is far greater than all these things.

It is easy to understand why anyone would find it difficult to think in a positive way when they encounter one problem after another, pushing them further and further into a state of despair. It is all very well to be told, 'Be positive!', but when you lack confidence you are consequently unable to think positively about your life. A person lacking in confidence and motivation has probably spent a lifetime creating the fragile foundations upon which life is built, so transforming a life that is uncertain and weak into one that is positive and strong seems a near impossibility.

Once negative habits have been allowed to internally crystallize, they will gradually solidify into external situations and circumstances. Changing the habits of a lifetime is extremely difficult, but certainly not impossible.

When you are worried or anxious about something which is generally impairing the quality of your life, you probably find some comfort in sitting and relaxing for a few moments, quietly turning the problem over in your mind, and exploring all the ways in which your predicament might be resolved. But more often than not, somewhere along the line, the imagination takes control, creating emotions which eventually convince you that things are definitely going to get worse. There is far more truth in the old saying, 'You will worry yourself into an early grave', than you might imagine. It therefore makes sense that if you are able to worry yourself into an early grave, the same principles must apply to thinking your way to good health, success and happiness.

I mentioned earlier that thoughts are living things, and that we are all pulled along by the thoughts and desires which we have previously set in motion. However, when struggling in the mire of self-created despair and panic, the only way to free yourself from such negative conditions is for you to realize that these dark emotions have no real connection with your problems other than the connection you yourself make with them.

Worrying about situations and events that have not yet happened quite often hastens their approach, and makes the thinker vulnerable and more susceptible to other similar situations and events. This is the Law of Attraction, and an understanding of it puts you in control of your own destiny. After all, you are the architect of your own destiny just by the way you think.

The way forward is to create new images in the imagination and to set these free, rather like large, helium-filled balloons floating off into space. You must create more than one image – don't forget that you have probably taken a lifetime to flood your life with worry and despair, so the first move forward must be with the positive realization that within you there exists the power that can now set you free. You must look upon the universe as a huge, treasure-filled grotto; send out a request to the universe for the things you require, and it will give you exactly what you want, in a very short time, as long as you believe in the Law of Attraction and that you really do have the power. A little understanding of this law will help you to move quicker and further through all your problems, regardless of what they are – health, financial, emotional, career, it doesn't matter. The universe is like the genie and the magic lamp; remember, *'Your wish is my command!'*

Those of you who have made a study of meditation, and explored the possibilities of mind power, will know that the electrical impulses produced by the brain change somewhat when certain meditative states are reached. These electrical impulses can be measured by connecting you to an electroencephalograph (EEG), when you are meditating, which measures and records the cyclic changes of electricity which occur in the brain during meditation. This offers us conclusive evidence that meditation is capable of producing measurable changes in the brain's activity.

A deep meditative state is often referred to as the *alpha state*, the term used to describe the brainwave patterns produced by meditation. This state has a much wider effect upon the physiological make-up of the person and can alleviate anxiety and stress, as well as encourage a whole new perspective on life.

The alpha state is also reached during sleep – when totally relaxed, or even when daydreaming. However, as there are often different levels to one's sleep patterns, the electrical energies produced by the brain also vary, and move from alpha to theta and to delta. Being fully awake and getting on with life's daily chores is performed while the brain is in beta, in which state numerous different feelings are experienced, depending entirely upon how the day is going for us.

The positive transformation of one's life must first of all begin with the certain knowledge that *you do possess the power to transform it*. Such a transformation involves the process of burning out the negative images that furnish your life, and which you have created over a lifetime of wrong thinking, and the creation of new and more positive images, giving them enough energy to sustain and perpetuate. To begin with you must eradicate the habit that we are all probably guilty of, and that is complaining about your problems, aches and pains and poor health. Talking about these things simply helps to perpetuate them and, in the long term, makes them worse. Create a new affirmation to be chanted daily, morning and night, such as 'I am healthy, wealthy, happy, successful and wise!'. Never say, 'I want to be healthy...'. This simply reflects your weakness and inability to transform the way you think, and makes your problems more important than they really are. You have to believe in the Law of Attraction and that the universe is most definitely there for you to call upon.

You may wonder what all this has to do with the process of psychic development? Well, the whole process of cultivating psychic skills is connected in many ways with mental control and the realization that you have a power that can transform your life in more ways than one. Once you have become totally focused on the powers within your mind, with the sole intention of cultivating awareness, the polarity of your life will change accordingly. During the process of psychic development, you must be prepared to feel 'different', and the way you handle that difference is solely dependent on your depth of understanding and awareness. It was once said: 'Psychic development is the process of creating a heaven using the materials of heaven itself.' This may sound paradoxical, but it is perhaps a precept that illustrates psychic development perfectly well.

Now, let us explore some methods for clearing and programming the subconscious mind with the sole intention of making you a more positive individual.

Exercise 28

- Try to relax totally, either sitting in a comfortable chair or lying on the bed. Close your eyes and 'see' your life as it presently is, with the usual worries, problems and anxieties. For a few moments allow yourself to relive each of these negative mental states, allowing your mind to go over all the things which present a problem for you, and mentally create a grey balloon around each one. Don't worry too much if you have difficulty visualizing the balloons perfectly, your intention is all that is really required at this point.

- Continue this process until you more or less have a clear picture in your imagination of yourself clutching the strings to which the grey balloons are attached.

- In your imagination, see yourself in control of the balloons, and when you are quite ready, release them with a smile. As they float off into the air, again using the power of your imagination, *will* them to return to you, and once again take hold of the strings.

- Hold the balloons for a few moments, reaffirming what is contained within them, ensuring that the balloons still represent each of your problems.

- Release them once again, and watch them float off into the air. Allow them to move a little further away than before, then again draw them back towards you, mentally taking hold of the strings. The whole mental process of releasing the balloons and then pulling them back is primarily to allow your subconscious mind to assert control over your problems and difficulties. Although a laborious process, it helps to cultivate mental strength and discipline, prerequisites for building up a more positive and dynamic you.

- You should continue the process of releasing and drawing back the balloons for as long as it takes for you to feel comfortable with the exercise. The whole mental process may seem quite ridiculous to you, but it does help in the cultivation of that part of the mind that you have never used before, and which really does contain the power that is there for you to use.

- When you feel confident that you fully understand the object of the exercise, and have begun to feel as though you have mastered the power to control your problems, you can consider the next phase of the exercise.

- Although the cause of your worry and despair is objective, the actual feelings themselves are created subjectively. It is therefore at a subliminal level that the work must take place.

- Now, seeing the balloons very clearly in your mind, reach out and mentally burst each one, allowing a moment to elapse between each impact. Be mindful of the fact that the destruction of the balloons is accompanied by the destruction of your worry and despair. Sit for a few moments relaxing before considering the next phase.

I am not suggesting for one moment that this exercise of the imagination will magically eradicate your financial difficulties, health problems, or any other seemingly insurmountable obstacle that you may be encountering in your everyday life, nor am I suggesting that you should ignore these problems completely. On the contrary, life is difficult enough without adding complications. However, by learning to master the immense powers within you, you may exert a more positive control over your life, enabling you to become the master. Such dramatic transformation of self has a much wider effect, not only on your mental life, but also on your physical and spiritual lives.

- Moving onto the next phase, allow your body to relax even more by breathing slowly and deeply, ensuring that the inhalations and exhalations are evenly spaced.

- Clear your mind completely. Feel yourself sinking into a state of sleep, totally relaxed and overwhelmed with a beautiful sense of peace and calm.

- When you feel relaxed enough, allow your imagination to light up the screen in your mind.

- Now, focus totally on those things that you desire, such as prosperity, health, happiness and peace of mind. Place each in order of its importance to you.

- Mentally create a brightly lit white balloon around each, and once again take hold of the strings to which they are attached.

- Allow your imagination to focus on each balloon, being

totally mindful of what that balloon represents.

- See the balloons glowing in your imagination, gleaming brightly as they float in the air in front of you.

- Look into each of the balloons and see the things you desire written very clearly in brightly coloured words.

- Now, as you did with the grey balloons, release them, allowing them to float upward. Watch them move away from you; then, using the strength and powers of your imagination once again, mentally draw them slowly back towards you.

- When they are close enough, mentally reach out, take hold of the strings and pull the balloons nearer to you. Once again check the contents of each balloon, reaffirming what they contain.

- Mentally infuse each balloon with more energy, making them glow even brighter and ensuring that you can see them clearly.

- Repeat this process over and over again, until you feel confident that you have them all under your control. Should you still be unsure of the measure of your control over the balloons and what they represent, leave the exercise, and come back to it later.

- When you fully understand the object of the exercise, and you feel confident about your control over the balloons, consider all the balloons and the feelings, desires and emotions they represent, and create a word which can encapsulate them collectively. The word can be anything, and take any form you like, as long as it is a word that you fully understand.

- Once you have created your word, focus on it for as long as it takes to fix it firmly in your mind. Remember that you have created this word and therefore understand the power behind it. In fact, look upon this word as your 'power word'. Explore the word fully, occasionally allowing your thoughts to reconsider the things that it represents for you.

- When you have total confidence in this word, and what is contained within it, allow your imagination to return to the white balloons. See them clearly in front of you, and then one by one, destroy them completely, making them disappear from your imagination.

- Now, move on to the next phase. Again, relax your body as deeply as you possibly can, clearing all residual images from your mind, and allowing yourself to drift once again to the point of sleep.

- Say to yourself, 'I will not sleep; I will only allow myself to be as totally relaxed as I possibly can.' Repeat this, breathing in and out slowly and deeply.

- Once you have found a feeling of complete serenity, allow the little screen in your mind to light up once again.

- Place your chosen word on the screen so that you can see it clearly.

- You are now going to convert that word into three separate finger positions which, when executed, will enable you to instantly release the inherent forces of your original desires.

- First, familiarize yourself with the three separate movements that represent three different levels of achievement.

Movement One

- Place your index finger between your eyebrows for a brief moment. This movement will enable you to be assertive, confident and able to cope in any difficult situation.

- The movement of the index finger to the space between the brows increases your capacity to concentrate and to protect your personal magnetism, thereby affording you the confidence you require when under pressure. Interviews, starting a new career, exams, beginning new ventures, going it alone in business, using your powers of observation, solving problems, thinking things through; in other words, anything which requires you to be alert and attentive may be achieved with the movement of the index finger to the brow.

- This finger movement has a subliminal psychological effect upon the brow centre – Ajna – and will precipitate all the qualities required and which you have created in the mental exercise. Remember, it is a psychological process that will only work once your subconscious mind has been programmed with the exercise.

Movement Two

- Touch the tip of your nose briefly with the middle finger of your right hand to release your deeper magnetic powers, so enabling you to overcome financial problems, and to gain a greater and more positive control over your financial life. By touching the tip of your nose you can overcome loneliness and feelings of insecurity, increasing your powers to attract new friends, good health, wealth, and a greater sense of adventure. This finger position also helps you to become more patient, astute and meticulous, and will encourage the release of those inner magnetic powers, cultivating the 'Midas Touch' in all that you do.

- Once the technique has been fully mastered, this finger position helps to activate the channels of energy between the throat centre – Vishudda – and the brow centre – Ajna, affording you a greater and more powerful force of attraction. All the finger positions have to be practised over and over again until fully established in the subconscious. Only then will they work for you.

- The only cautionary note I would say here is that this finger position must not be used for selfish reasons, or to hurt others, because this may cause the opposite effect to be experienced, reintroducing all the original negative situations and emotions with a force far greater than before.

Movement Three

- Touch your throat briefly with the little finger of your right hand to release a surge of psychic power, allowing you to see things more clearly.

- This finger movement will make you more intuitive, and will also aid the self-healing process of those recovering from illness. It will precipitate creative and psychic skills, making them stronger and more dynamic. It helps to cultivate oratory abilities, making you more communicative and articulate and more able to convey your thoughts and feelings to others with far greater confidence and ease. This finger position releases the inherent powers of the throat centre – Vishudda – and affects your awareness and perception of objects, situations and people. It can also be of assistance when you are struggling with a lack of discipline.

The finger positions themselves will have no effect at all unless the accompanying visualization exercise has been followed and practised regularly. To enable them to really work for you a programme has to be created first.

There is a strong chance that when you first read through the whole of this exercise you will dismiss it purely upon the grounds that it seems so complicated and laborious. However, the primary object of the technique is to re-programme your subconscious mind, in an effort to encourage you to be more positive and dynamic. On this basis it would be advisable for you to read through it a few times before actually attempting it, thus firmly fixing the technique fully in your mind.

It is a good idea also to make a list of all the things you would like to change in your life and all the things you want to achieve before attempting the exercise.

Although the exercise in creative visualization is important in making the finger positions work for you, try not to make it too complicated for yourself. Keep the quantity of imaginary balloons in the exercises to a minimum; you may even allow the balloons to contain more than one thing.

You will also find it of value to the results and effectiveness of the finger positions if you associate each balloon with one of them. For example, one or two balloons may contain a desire for wealth and happiness, in that case focus on the appropriate balloons for a few moments, then apply the finger to the corresponding position, thereby setting the programme in motion.

It may be the case that you find it easier to modify the exercise in some way, in order to suit your own grasp and understanding of it. This will not adversely affect the results, as long as the creative imagery exercise has been practised until the programme has been fully established in your mind. Remember, it does take time and practice to make the exercise work for you, but you can rest assured that your perseverance and determination will produce positive results.

Even when the technique has been fully mastered it is a good idea to practise it as regularly as possible, in order to reintroduce the imagery into the subconscious and maintain its performance at a subconscious level.

It may also be that you want to re-programme the exercise occasionally, having achieved your previous aims. I would certainly suggest that you do this, as your abilities will benefit from an occasional 'clear out', just as though you were discarding an old and worn video tape and replacing it with a new and much clearer one.

Remember, the mind is a powerful entity and its performance can be greatly improved with exercise, just as the strength and power of the physical body can be enhanced by subjecting it to a rigorous training routine in the gym.

Chapter Eight

Psychic Self-Defence

The very suggestion of psychic attack is frequently dismissed as nonsense, even by some psychics, let alone by the non-psychic sceptic. The idea that you can be harmed, either mentally or physically, by another individual, without any physical contact taking place, has been known in many cultures for thousands of years, and today with the growing interest in all things of a paranormal nature, is something that is certainly becoming more of a reality. Working on the premise that a so-called psychic attack is possible, then it is always best to err on the side of caution by cultivating a method to protect yourself, should you find yourself the target for such an attack.

Generally speaking, because any psychic attack originates at a mental level, defending oneself from such a subtle invasion should also be conducted at a corresponding level. The mind is the common denominator where all things of a psychic nature are concerned, and so cultivating the powers within the mind is of paramount importance, particularly when dealing with psychic attack. More often than not, being aware of someone who is intent on psychically harming you very often empowers them. This might sound somewhat paradoxical, as such an attack nearly always catches the victim unawares, and so one might say that 'forewarned is forearmed'. Not as far as I am concerned, and I hope that by the end of this chapter you will understand exactly what I mean.

We are constantly being bombarded and influenced by the streams and waves of thoughts which have been created and then set in motion by minds both past and present, and we are often overwhelmed by the force of such thoughts, to the extent of being pulled into the mire of depression or occasionally encouraged to heights of greater fulfilment. I am of course talking about those subtle atmospheres we all experience from time to time in old buildings, or even in specific geographical areas. However, some people are more sensitive to these vibratory atmospheres than others. Nonetheless, regardless of whether or not one is sensitive, everyone is ultimately affected by the invisible forces that permeate the psychic atmosphere surrounding them, and which have the profound effect of flooding the mind with the emotions with which they were first created.

Although most psychic forces that are released into the atmosphere have no particular power behind them, the energies that permeate bricks-and-mortar structures and geographical locations do represent the minds of those who created them in the first place. These energies either warm and encourage us, or create feelings of foreboding and terror. How we are affected by the psychic atmosphere is solely dependent upon the character and personality of those who have been instrumental in creating it in the first place. If evil minds were the primary creators of the psychic atmosphere of an old house or even a particular location, then all those who come within the confines of its radiations will most certainly be affected.

As I have previously said, thoughts are living things; the stronger and more intense the thought, the more energy is contained within it. The more energy present with each thought, the longer that thought will persist in the psychic atmosphere. Districts, towns, cities and even nations are permeated by the thoughts of those who live or have lived there. The various waves of thought hover in the psychic space, in very much the same way that clouds fall into groups in the atmosphere. These waves of thought energies are of different degrees of vibration, and so the same space may be filled with thought matter of a thousand kinds, interpenetrating each other, without interference. The anguish and despair of a nation stricken by famine and war simply infuses the looming negative energies with even more anguish and despair, thus perpetuating the plight of those who dwell there. An old house with a cold and unfriendly atmosphere will remain so until the energies which have impregnated the subtle nature of the bricks and mortar over the years have been reversed.

Although everyone is affected by subtle, atmospheric energies, to some greater or lesser degree, those who have a propensity towards being psychic are more inclined to be influenced by them. Although the majority of those working in the psychic field do possess strong principles, and work to a strict code of practice, there is a minority who have a complete disregard of others, and simply use their psychic skills for the gratification of their own desires and passions. Such individuals are usually very aware of the power they possess and know exactly how to use it. It is therefore of paramount importance that those working in the psychic field should always be mindful of the fact that they, more than anyone else, are susceptible to psychic attack either from incarnate minds or even disembodied minds, the vagabonds and rogues who roam menacingly through the lower vibratory planes of the astral world seeking to gratify the lower passions and desires for evil.

No matter what the source of the attack, the techniques of protection must ultimately be the same, and measures must therefore be taken immediately to create some form of positive protection. Continuous psychic attack can eventually wear down the levels of resistance to such a degree as to be extremely detrimental to one's health. By infiltrating the psychic's aura, the invading thought-forces gradually gain access to the mind and are then able to influence the psychic practitioner against their will.

A perpetrator of a psychic attack often possesses the power to influence the victim remotely and, when such an attack is sustained for long periods, it can cause the victim serious health problems.

Although I accept the existence of spirit guides, etc, it would be irresponsible for any working psychic to wrongly assume that he or she is totally protected by such beings. Waiting for such an attack to take place before creating the protection is like closing the gate after the horse has bolted. I would suggest that you always work on the premise that a psychic attack is going to take place, and to formulate a protective programme as soon as you even consider embarking upon metaphysical studies.

Furthermore, it is not always when you are awake that an attack may take place. Indeed, most 'psychic attacks' come when one is asleep and therefore most vulnerable. In this way the invading forces are able to meet you on their own ground, so to speak, in the lower regions of the astral world, where their mal-evolence is most powerful and able to exercise the greatest force.

Such attacks can be detrimental to the psychological make-up, and although the techniques of protection are more or less the same, the approach is slightly different inasmuch as specific *thought forms* need to be created with a particular mission in mind.

Whatever area of the psychic field you work in, a healthy and well-balanced approach is of great importance. There is no place for fanciful notions such as thinking that because your intentions are good and honourable you will automatically be afforded divine protection. Nor is there any place for ignorance and the belief that just because you do not know about it, harm will not come to you.

A great deal of nonsense is talked about psychic self-defence, and about what one ought and ought not to do. It is true that we are looked upon and guided to some extent by angelic forces, but it must also be understood that *they* are only as strong and as powerful as your weakest point, and they may even guide you into a difficult situation whereby you can attain greater knowledge and experience.

While you sleep, and the physical senses are more or less anaesthetized to feeling, the consciousness functions, to some greater or lesser degree, in the astral body, and it is through this body's corresponding senses that knowledge and information are obtained about the astral world. The majority of people do not have any recollection of their sojourn in the astral sleep state, but those who do remember find that their experiences mostly filter through into the conscious mind after having been transmuted into the symbolization of dreams. However, it would be ridiculous to suppose that all dreams represent the symbolic results of astral experiences, as the majority of our dreams are merely the results of overindulgence of one kind or another, or even the mind's natural process of dealing with stress and anxiety.

A recurring dream, however, is definitely the result of an astral experience, and may fit into one of two categories. The first is of a prophetic nature, and is usually termed a 'precognitive dream'. This is a dream from which prophetic information is gleaned, and which usually comes true in time. The second type of dream often reveals the dreamer in some dangerous situation, or even being attacked and then killed. It is also quite common in this sort of dream to see oneself as being dead and sometimes laid out in a coffin. A dream of this nature is almost certainly the result of some sort of psychic attack, and it will certainly continue to recur until something is done to prevent it.

A recurring dream featuring an assault upon the dreamer by some form of demon often means that malevolent forces have been set against them. In order to deal with this unfortunate and extremely frightening case a specific *thought form* needs to be created over a period of time. This should be released into the astral space each night before going asleep. The most vulnerable time for the sleeper is during the hypnogogic and hypnopompic states; the first being the process of drifting into sleep, and the second when the consciousness is beginning to awaken. It is during these two cognitive states that access can easily be gained by evil forces that will seize the opportunity to either attack or gain control of the victim's consciousness. I am aware that all this may sound like something straight from the pages of a Denis Wheatley book, but the dangers are very real and must not be taken too lightly.

The following process will help:

Psychic Self-Defence: Method One

- Each night before you go to sleep, lie quietly on your bed with your eyes fixed on a certain spot on the ceiling.

- Begin to breathe rhythmically, slowly and deeply, making sure that the inhalations and exhalations are evenly spaced.

- Resist the temptation to blink, but when the eyes tear and move out of focus, slowly close them but do not allow yourself to fall asleep.

- Feel overwhelmed with a sense of peace, and create in your mind a beautiful pool of pulsating blue light, the kind that colours a clear blue sky on a summer's day.

- Let this pool of blue light be full of movement, almost alive.

- See it very clearly in your mind, and imagine it almost filling your bedroom, surrounding you as you lie on the bed.

- Across the surface of this pool of blue light create a golden equidistant cross, whose intersecting lines establish four points of contact at the circumference of the pool. In this way your sacred pool of blue light is sealed by the power of the equidistant cross.

- See yourself lying in the centre of this pool and allow the blue light to surround you.

- Now physically extend your arms (not just in your mind), and imagine yourself lying on the cross.

- Feel the golden rays emanating from it and passing through you.

- Do not permit your mind to wander even for a moment from this picture of yourself and the pool, and resist any temptation to fall asleep.

- Feel yourself becoming totally submerged in the pulsating pool of blue light, and mentally say to yourself five times: 'This is the sacred pool and I am filled with the power of the golden cross. No harm shall come to me.'

Recreate the sacred pool of blue light each night before you go to sleep, and eventually your dreams should be free of malevolence. Even if you lack the power to visualize, it is important that you feel that you are actually there. In this way your subconscious mind is infused with the power of the imagery. However, should no change occur in your dreams, you should move to the second step.

Psychic Self-Defence: Method Two

- Each night, before you recreate your sacred pool, spend a few minutes lying peacefully in a relaxed position, breathing slowly and gently, until the mind is totally serene and quiet.

- Imagine yourself being looked upon by a tall, strong, friendly figure whose form towers over you in a protective stance. This figure can take any form you like, as long as it is strong and powerful, and possesses an overwhelming feeling of friendship and belonging to you. You may not wish to create a human form; a powerful animal such as a bear or lion or something similar will suffice, as long as you feel comfortable and protected by it and know it will always be there to keep away any unwanted entities. In fact, this is the first step to creating a thought form that will always protect you.

- Once you have created your protective thought form, begin to recreate your sacred pool of blue light in front of it.

- While you picture yourself lying on the golden cross in the sacred pool, see yourself being looked upon by your friend and protector.

- Spend as long as it takes to familiarize yourself with the exercise, then allow yourself to drift gently into the realms of slumber, to dream peaceful dreams without threat or fear of any danger.

- I would also add that you must know everything about your silent protector. Memorize the features, the shape of the face, the eyes and nose. Know every characteristic, every feeling and even endeavour to create a personal fragrance peculiar to your protector.

• Animate it and endow it with intelligence. Talk to it and imagine it responding telepathically. Over the nights that follow, programme your protector by telling it to guide and protect you while you sleep and also while you go about your daily routine. Build your relationship slowly, until you feel a deep affinity with it.

Please do not dismiss these methods as being ridiculous. The main object of the exercise is to programme your subconscious mind so that it will always be alert and in control. The fundamental principles underlying the art of psychic self-defence are a strong and active imagination, a disciplined mind, and a strong and vibrant *will power.*

The only cautionary note I would like to add is to create your silent protector in your mind only while you are in your bedroom preparing to sleep. This is a vital part of the programming and should be consistent. In this way your thought form knows that it is to follow you into sleep, and in those realms it must remain by your side relentlessly. Of course, once such a thought form has been created and fully established in the consciousness, it will remain there silently watching over you throughout the day as well as the night.

• •

It is quite difficult for some people to understand just how effective such an exercise in mind power can actually be. The 'things' encountered during sleep are often menacingly created out of potent materials and substances of the lower astral planes. It is from these very materials and substances, therefore, that the weapons to protect oneself must ultimately be created.

It is also a good idea to repeat mentally a prayerful affirmation, such as the Lord's Prayer, or one you have composed yourself. In any case, do not underestimate the power and potency of prayer, regardless of your belief.

When one has been continuously subjected to psychic attack the aura becomes sluggish and fragmented, particularly around the head and solar plexus areas. Some psychic attacks are so subtle that the victim is sometimes unaware of exactly what is happening, and may in fact put the manifestations of such an attack down to illness or simply being run-down. Headaches, depression and lethargy may all be the result of psychic attack and if ignored may, in time, cause serious mental illness. Should you harbour the slightest suspicion that you may be on the receiving end of some kind of psychic attack, do something about it right away. When you are working in the psychic field you should always work on the premise that you are a target and always take precautions to alleviate the situation. Formulate a working programme of constructive visualization as soon as possible and, if necessary, consult someone who possesses knowledge of the subject.

It is also a good idea to abstain from drinking alcohol, at least until you feel that you have the situation under control. Alcohol and drugs weaken the subtle anatomy, making the aura more susceptible to psychic attack. Those with addictive personalities are prime targets for some sort of disembodied infiltration, as their dependency, no matter how slight, is indicative of mental and personality weakness, which provides easy prey for those seeking either to destroy or to control you via psychic means.

Mentally, one should always be on one's guard when working psychically and also be conscious at all times of every aspect of one's life. It is not always the intention of the psychic attacker to invade a person's physical body or, for that matter, their mind.

There are some who have the power to affect negative changes in another's life by bringing chaos to it. A psychic attack is very subtle and can certainly take many forms. It is sometimes so powerful as to exert great control over the circumstances of an individual's life, and may interfere with, or destroy relationships and the overall equilibrium of one's life. I am speaking from experience here, as I personally know only too well just what powerful forces can be in operation when one is subject to a psychic attack.

From time to time it is a good idea to cleanse the aura with a simple yet effective exercise using the following method.

Psychic Self-Defence: Method Three

Rhythmic breathing should be an integral part of all your psychic training. This not only makes the mind quiet, but it also encourages movement in the chakras and infuses the aura with vitality.

- Sit in a relaxed position in a comfortable chair. Breathe rhythmically until the rhythm is fully established in your mind and you feel relaxed.

- In your mind create a curtain of blue light, beginning from the floor by your feet, all the way up to the ceiling above your head.

- Light up the curtain of blue with sparkling rays of silver which are bright and shiny, rather like currents of electricity moving along a bare connection.

- Feel the blue energies against your body and allow this curtain of blue light to overwhelm you.

- Draw the blue light in through your nostrils and down into your body until you feel filled with blue light.

• Very slowly, change the curtain of blue light to red, and allow the red curtain of light to envelope you as completely as possible.

• Feel the warmth of the red energy against your skin, and see these vibrations burning away all the negative energy in your aura.

• Feel the red energy pulsating inside you, and see yourself being completely revitalized.

• Hold this image for a few moments, and then gradually change the red curtain of energy to a golden curtain. Feel invigorated by the golden rays of light, which fill your whole being, elevating your consciousness. Hold it for a few moments, and then very slowly allow the whole exercise to slowly fade. Relax in your chair for a few minutes, allowing your mind to review the exercise.

These methods are exercises in mental imagery, so therefore need to be practised regularly in order to establish them fully in the mind.

The effects of this exercise may not be fully appreciated immediately, but as time passes you will begin to feel mentally stimulated and more grounded. It also has a remarkable cleansing effect upon the practitioner's aura, making the colours appear more vibrant and clear. The psychological implications are quite amazing and will have a profound effect upon the mind. Of course, the results of this sort of treatment only become more permanent when it is practised regularly, over a period of time. In itself the exercise should not be looked upon as a method of psychic self-defence, but more as an exercise to cleanse psychic germs from the aura.

In this respect it is also helpful to drink a few glasses of psychically charged water. As I said on page 32 and elsewhere, water should be charged simply by passing it from one glass to another, over and over again, until the water appears almost to sparkle with vitality. The water will take on the appearance of almost being 'alive' with vitality, and it will taste like fresh mountain spring water.

• •

Other, more specific methods of psychic self-defence appear on the surface to be very general, but in fact they take a great deal of patience and concentration. The art of visualization does not come easily to everyone, but unfortunately it is a prerequisite in one's endeavours to create protective barriers.

The following method is one that can be used in most cases of psychic attack, and it will also strengthen the practitioner's powers of resistance. The exercise itself is quite easy to follow, but it does call for a great deal of dedication. It must be explored fully to enable the practitioner to comprehend the depth of its true meaning. Once the technique has been mastered you will find yourself standing on the threshold of a profound spiritual experience.

• •

Psychic Self-Defence: Method Four

- Find a quiet corner and sit in a comfortable chair. It may be a good idea to burn some pleasant incense, any fragrance which is pleasing to your senses.

- With your eyes closed begin to breathe slowly and deeply, allowing your stomach to rise as you breathe in, and letting it fall as you breathe out. Breathe in this way for five to ten minutes, ensuring that you do not make it a labour, and then relax with your eyes closed.

- Be aware of the space surrounding you, and feel that you are a part of that space. Feel that you are merely occupying your body temporarily, and that you may, therefore, leave it at any time you desire, knowing that you must always return to it when the exercise is over.

- See the space surrounding you as sacred and holy ground, an area which no one, whether seen or unseen, can enter.

- Allow the space surrounding you to become slowly flooded with vibrant light, coloured with pink.

- Feel overwhelmed with pink energy, and allow it to infuse your mind, your heart and your soul with gentleness, compassion and love.

- Make your surrounding space strong and impenetrable, by creating a high wall of golden light around its circumference. Infuse the wall with more energy, making it even more vibrant and powerful.

- Feel yourself totally submerged in the surrounding pink light, and know, without any shadow of a doubt, that this is your space, your sacred and holy space, in which nothing and no one can move.

I cannot emphasize enough just how important the imagery is in this sort of exercise. Should the mind wander even for a moment it will break the spell, so to speak, and cease to be as effective. Before attempting any of the exercises given it is a good idea if you read through them a few times, firmly fixing them in your mind. As with the other exercises, this must also be practised regularly to enable one's confidence in its effectiveness to develop. Should you only half believe in the protective powers of any of the exercises, their effectiveness will be lessened. Know that they do work, and believe in their power and potency.

For general psychic protection many people simply use the *auric egg* method. This can also be very effective.

Psychic Self-Defence: Method Five

- First of all, decide which colour you feel is powerful enough to afford you the spiritual protection. It should of course be one with which you also feel comfortable. Then create an auric egg of this colour around yourself.

- See yourself objectively at first, sitting completely surrounded by the colour of choice. Then, very slowly allow the colour to obliterate you completely, until you can only see the coloured egg before you.

- At this point feel yourself inside the egg, with plenty of movement in the colour, allowing the energy to infuse you with vitality, to the extent that you can feel yourself almost vibrate.

- Continue this visualization for ten minutes. Thereafter it should be practised every day.

There is always the danger that because of an exercise's simplicity you will dismiss it as not being very effective. I cannot stress enough the importance of your belief in the exercises you use. Once the image-making faculty of the brain well and truly connects with the imagery you create in it, the subconscious mind then becomes programmed, thus encouraging the full power of the exercise to be released. These are the fundamental principles of visualization and mind power, prerequisites for the process of psychic development.

Anyone working in the psychic field should always look upon themselves as being *carriers of light*. Always be mindful that there are those, both in this world and the next, whose sole intention it is to prevent light from moving into this world. See yourself as a soldier constantly walking beyond enemy lines, remaining ever vigilant. This might sound ridiculous to some, who will probably feel inclined to pour scorn on what I have said. But believe me: experience alone will make the truth of what I have said clear to you.

Psychic Self Defence: Method Six

Should you be fortunate enough to own some sort of pyramid structure in which to meditate, so much the better for this method of psychic protection. Otherwise you will need to mentally create one.

- As before, sit comfortably and breathe rhythmically, with your eyes closed, until the rhythm is fully established in your mind.

- See yourself standing outside a pyramid – a golden pyramid silhouetted against a clear blue sky. See the pyramid shimmering with energy, its walls translucent, rather like mother-of-pearl.

- In your mind watch the energy pouring through the apex of the pyramid, and see it coming alive.

- There is no entrance in the pyramid, so you must simply allow yourself to pass through one of its shimmering walls and then find yourself inside. You may do so because it is constructed from pure energy alone and is constantly vibrating. Sit in your pyramid for a few moments imbibing the power and vitality. On the wall of the pyramid facing you there is a large eye staring at you. Make the eye friendly and reassuring.

- Clasp your hands on your lap and repeat mentally: 'Oh magic and all-seeing eye, protect me and make me wise. In my endeavours, watch over me all through my day and in my sleep.' Again, I must stress the importance of the imagery. Do not allow your attention to wander, even for a single moment.

- Remain sitting in your pyramid for ten minutes longer. Feel totally calm and strong. Then mentally step out through the wall, stand back and look at the pyramid. Slowly allow the exercise to dissolve, clearing it completely from your mind. Wait a few moments then open your eyes.

- It is always a good idea to conclude any meditative visualization with some rhythmic breathing. This helps to clear the mind and close everything down.

Although most of these exercises are quite simple, their effectiveness is dependent on the actual discipline of practice, and the total realization of what exactly is involved in the exercise, as well as the overwhelming belief that it will work. The mind is most certainly the common denominator, and you are only as strong as your weakest thought. Through the creative energies of the mind the most powerful weapons are forged.

Certain crystals, too, can be used in a ritualistic approach to psychic protection. The amethyst is sometimes referred to as the *spiritual stone*, and simply holding a piece in the hands produces a calming effect upon the mind. Its inherent properties help to encourage serenity and peace of mind, and also the precipitation of any latent psychic and spiritual abilities. Being the spiritual stone, it is also an ideal source of protection.

The electromagnetic energies of crystals allow them to be easily programmed. Once programmed in the way I have explained, the amethyst is capable of releasing amazing powerful energies. Its subtle spiritual properties often encourage the gentle stone to draw to itself the possessor's problems, burdens, dangers and fears. In fact, when a person is overwhelmed with problems the amethyst has been known to crack or even shatter as a direct result of drawing to itself the negative forces experienced by the owner.

The clear quartz crystal is an extremely powerful stone. Resilient and dynamic, it is often known as the *enhancing stone*, simply because it has the incredible power to increase the energy in anything close to it. Because of its inherent 'psychic' properties, the clear quartz has always been used as a focal point for concentration, and has been used from time immemorial as the powerful crystal from which the crystal ball is made, the divinatory tool favoured by many ancient Romany seers who would use it to glean information about the future. The clear quartz crystal also emanates a powerful protective energy and, combined with the amethyst, is able to create an incredibly powerful barrier against negative evil forces.

For this particular method you will need four clear quartz pointers and one fairly good quality piece of amethyst.

• •

Psychic Self-Defence: Method Seven

Before beginning this exercise you must first programme your crystals. Wash them in a saline solution (salt water), and add a little cider vinegar. Rinse them thoroughly under a running cold tap, and then leave them to dry naturally in the sunlight. This process cleanses the crystals of other people's vibrations, touch and personal fragrances.

To programme the crystals, simply place them in your cupped hands on your lap, and sit comfortably in a quiet corner. Meditate upon your crystals, expressing your wishes and mentally infusing them with your will and motives. Spend 10 to 15 minutes on this, then wrap your crystals in a clean white linen cloth and place them somewhere safe, not to be touched by anyone but yourself.

The white cloth is important. Black absorbs emotion and the negative energies of others, while white reflects these, and is of course pure. Try also to keep your crystals away from bright sunlight and other people. Treat them in an almost reverential way, as though they are human and possess sacred qualities. Treating your crystals in this way endows them with even more energy and supernatural power. Mentally speak to them in the quietness, tell them your fears and requirements. Ask them for protection at all times. Welcome their friendship and their guidance, and even ask them to impart their knowledge to you. Meditate upon them as frequently as possible, as this encourages their inherent qualities to be discharged.

- For this method, place your clear quartz crystals one in each corner of the room, the points directed towards the centre, where your chair should be.

- Sit quietly on your chair, relaxed but with your back straight, shoulders slightly back, and your hands resting, palms up, in your lap with the amethyst piece held lightly between the tips of your fingers.

- With your eyes closed, simply breathe in slowly and deeply, all the time being mindful of the amethyst piece in your hands.

- Focus your attention first of all on the amethyst stone, calling upon it to release its powers, its inherent properties.

- Be mindful of the clear quartz pointers in the corners of the room, and feel the energy emanating from them to you and penetrating your very being. Feel the clear quartz crystals creating a circuit of energy across and around the room. Be totally aware of this energy, which appears to pass through your body rather like electricity.

- Feel completely secure within the field of energy produced by all the crystals. This energy field appears to be drawn to the amethyst resting in your hands. Mentally feel your body glowing, almost alive with energy and power, and for a few moments experience a feeling of bliss, of 'at-one-ment' with the universal spirit or universal mind, and know without a doubt that nothing can inflict harm upon you.

- When you feel quite comfortable with the exercise and you can see and feel the energy moving freely around the room, create, in your mind, a dome of purple light and colour, and allow sunlight to filter through it and cascade down upon the amethyst piece in your hands.

- See the room aglow with colour and light, and as the sunshine filters through the dome of light to fall upon the amethyst, visualize it breaking up into innumerable colours, which in turn change into a myriad of even more beautiful colours falling about you like minute rainbows.

- Let the room be alive with colour, light and energy, and in the midst of it all feel a sense of peace overwhelming you.

- Sit for a few minutes longer, allowing this emotion to wash over you.

- As before, conclude the exercise with some rhythmic breathing, closing it all down completely.

As I have previously said, with exercises of this nature it is always a good idea to read through the instructions before attempting them, primarily to ensure that you have fixed them firmly in your mind and therefore know exactly what to do. Should you feel you need to modify the exercise in some way, then feel free! Do what is necessary to make you feel comfortable and able to use the exercise with ease and confidence.

This particular exercise is very effective for cleansing the aura and for stimulating the image-making faculty of the mind. It is also an effective method for the creation of a protective barrier when one is subject to a subliminal psychic attack.

Practise the exercise before going to sleep, then place the clear quartz pointers one at each corner of your bed, points towards each corner. Sleep with the amethyst under your pillow (but only for three nights) then when you wake, sit at the end of your bed with your eyes closed, holding the amethyst gently in your hands. Breathe in and out for a few moments, slowly and deeply, focusing your complete attention on the amethyst stone, and taking from it that which you require to sustain you throughout the day.

Try to begin each day with half a pint of fresh water. Energize it by pouring it from one vessel to another, over and over again, backward and forward until the water sparkles with vitality and energy. Drink it slowly to absorb the prana, and then relax for a few moments before beginning your day.

It probably would not be practical to practise this exercise every single day, and so it is better that you include it in your training programme when suitable for you. It would also not be very practical to use all the psychic protection methods together. You may prefer one particular method, or you may even choose to include more than one exercise in your training programme. As long as it works for you, do whatever you feel is necessary.

Chapter Nine

Out-of-Body Experience: Astral Projection

We hear a great deal these days about out-of-body experiences (OBEs). Claims are made by some that they have found themselves floating outside their physical body which they could see below them, either fast asleep in bed, or even lying on an operating table, surrounded by a medical team, undergoing surgery. Today there is far too much evidence to support these claims for us to dismiss the out-of-body experience as being ridiculous. Many such experiences have been documented over the last 20 years or so, involving people from many different walks of life, many nationalities, and diverse cultures and religious beliefs. Some of the accounts recorded have been given by people who allegedly have had no prior knowledge of such a phenomenon and have involved the elderly and even very young children.

Even though much of the information contained within the accounts of out-of-body experiences differs in various ways, all the reports have a common thread which binds them together in some way, thereby adding credence to the claims made.

Although most of the experiences occur mainly when the body is anaesthetized, there have been accounts of this unusual phenomenon taking place quite spontaneously while the person was fully awake. When this happens, the person can be left in very little doubt that it has occurred while they were fully awake. However, overactivity of the imagination can only be eliminated when the out-of-body experience has been put to the test. It must be said, however, that six out of ten cases fail this test miserably, even though it is quite straightforward. The person is simply asked to relate that which they observed during the out-of-body experience, which would not have otherwise been seen had their consciousness remained in the physical body. Furthermore, this person also experiences a heightened state of awareness of everything around them, so their consciousness is able to somehow transcend the limitations of the physical body to perceive a fuller geographical landscape. For example, allowing them to experience things taking place in an adjacent room or even road. One other factor common to all those who have had any sort of out-of-body phenomenon is that they find the experience extremely pleasant, and something which they would very much like to repeat.

Before we talk about techniques whereby one can produce such a phenomenon, we must first of all look at the reasons why it happens at all, and also explore the whole concept of the out-of-body phenomenon and its possibilities.

Even though the out-of-body experience may be considered a very natural phenomenon, it cannot in any way be thought of as 'normal', and it is certainly not the sort of event one experiences every day of the week. Although it is a phenomenon which can sometimes be indicative of certain psychological and emotional illnesses, it is not, strictly speaking, symptomatic of anything in particular. It is certainly a phenomenon that is being widely studied today, and one over which modern-day psychologists seem to be more or less split in their opinions, although nearly all are in agreement that such a phenomenon does indeed exist.

Before we explore the out-of-body experience, we must first of all work on the premise that man not only possesses an astral body in the first place, but that he himself is an extremely complex being, possessing other more subtle bodies through which his consciousness can also move and have experience. In theory, man can experience awareness of these bodies at any time, and sometimes does, without actually realizing it. For example, consider a soldier in the grip of attack behind enemy lines. His consciousness is completely focused upon the approaching enemy and the battle at hand, and he does not notice that he has been wounded. Once the battle is over and the enemy has withdrawn, his consciousness is once again drawn towards his physical body and, realizing that he has been injured, he falls into unconsciousness. During the time the soldier's consciousness was preoccupied he experienced awareness in one of his astral counterparts, thus making the physical body completely anaesthetized to all sensation, and therefore oblivious to anything other than the approaching danger. Although an extremely simple analogy, it is, I feel, one which illustrates the concept of shifting consciousness perfectly well.

Another example is that experienced in deep sleep when one is dreaming. Here, again, the sleeper is completely oblivious to both his body and his surroundings, and experiences awareness in a state of consciousness over which he appears to have little or no control. If the sleeper were able to control his consciousness during the time he was asleep, there would be limitless possibilities and great freedom of awareness available to him. By cultivating greater control of the consciousness, particularly during the sleep state, man would be able to access states of awareness in which time and space as we conceive them to be would simply not exist. I am, of course, speaking of the 'subjective' levels of the astral world, in which the geography is peculiar to that part of the astral universe alone and in no way bears any relation to the geography of the physical world.

Because of the very nature of the astral world, until one

develops the ability of the consciousness to function with a more controlled freedom in it, one's sensory awareness of the astral world can only be described as nebulous. However, once such development takes place, it is as though a grey veil rises to reveal before the consciousness a new and vibrant landscape of colour, form and sound.

As your awareness of the astral world develops during the initial stages, you should have a deeper awareness of the hypnogogic state – when the consciousness hovers between being awake and being asleep – before finally entering the sleep state. The hypnopompic experience – just before waking up – should also produce vivid memory experiences, once the astral technique you use starts to take effect.

Various techniques can be employed to help with the projection of the astral body, but before any of these are explored one should learn to focus the consciousness upon the *self* in a simple meditative exercise.

Technique One
Step One

- Sit in a relaxed posture, preferably on a straight-backed chair, ensuring that your chest, neck and head are as nearly in a straight line as possible, with your shoulders thrown slightly back and your hands resting lightly on your lap.

- Breathe rhythmically until the rhythm is fully established in your mind, making quite sure that the inhalations and exhalations are evenly spaced. The importance of rhythmic breathing when endeavouring to develop astral consciousness cannot be stressed enough here, as the control of your breathing enhances awareness on all levels of consciousness.

- Make the mind as quiet as possible as you continue to breathe in and out.

- Remain in this position for a few minutes, until you are totally relaxed, then rise from your chair and walk into an adjacent room.

- Take note of everything you can see there, making a clear picture in your mind so that you know where everything is positioned, and can recall it in your imagination later.

- Return to your chair in your quiet room and relax once again.

- Begin to breathe slowly and deeply, summoning all the power you can into your solar plexus.

- Discharge this power on the exhalations, while creating in your mind a clear image of yourself standing in front of you and yet facing the other way, so that you have a clear view of your back.

- Try to see yourself clearly, dressed in the same clothes that you are wearing now, and watch yourself walking away towards the door.

- When you can see yourself reaching the door, freeze the image of yourself, breathe in deeply, and on the exhalation allow the image of yourself to fade.

Step Two

- Rise from your chair and wander once again into the adjacent room. Repeat the motions of looking round and checking the position of everything in the room. Use all your senses to accurately record the full picture.

• Familiarize yourself with any fragrances, pay attention to colours, and make a special note of the exact position of furniture. In other words, refresh your mental picture of exactly how everything looks. Now return to your chair in your quiet room and relax again, with your eyes closed.

• Breathe slowly and deeply once more, paying attention to the streams of vitality flowing in through your nostrils and down into your solar plexus. Remember, as you breathe in let your stomach rise, and when you breathe out let it fall. Each time you exhale, discharge the power, simultaneously recreating the mental image of yourself standing in the doorway ready to leave. See yourself passing through the door and out of sight.

• The image-making faculty of the mind is a primary key to the precipitation of the astral body, and combined with rhythmic breathing makes the mental imagery clearer and more defined. Remember, access to the astral world is obtained subjectively, and so your powers of visualization are of paramount importance. If you have difficulty visualizing, this must be cultivated before separation of the astral body can effectively take place.

• Still totally relaxed, now mentally picture yourself standing there. Allow yourself mentally to move into the adjacent room. Once there, stand for a few moments and look around. Project your consciousness and feel as though you are actually there: smell the fragrances, see the colours of everything around you, and note the position of the furniture. Move about in the room, allowing your eyes to scan your surroundings, before slowly moving back towards the door.

- Mentally stand in the doorway for a few moments and take a look around before leaving the room and returning to your chair. Before opening your eyes sit quietly for a few moments, breathing gently and rhythmically. When you feel ready to conclude the exercise breathe in deeply one last time, and with the exhalation discharge the whole picture from your mind, and then open your eyes.

- Once you have finished it is vitally important not to go over the exercise in your mind. Instead, direct your mind completely away from it, and then make yourself a warm drink.

Initially, the primary object of these exercises is to cultivate the ability to use your imagination as a vehicle of conveyance, and to project your consciousness from one place to another. There is an art to this and some people may find it very difficult. However, with time and perseverance you will master the technique of mind travel and then discover the key to astral projection. Even if your powers of imagination are extremely good, little will be accomplished from one or two attempts at the exercises. To achieve full astral projection the experiment must be conducted over and over until very little concentration is needed on your part, and the imagery is processed of its own accord, without any effort at all. When this happens you will know it instantly as everything will appear so vivid and clearly defined. The imagery you create in your mind will suddenly become intensified and you should then experience a pleasurable feeling of floating. This is the all-important point at which the astral body seeks separation. When this sensation is experienced the majority of people become excited, inhibiting the process so that it simply does not progress any further. Once you experience this sensation of buoyancy try to remain completely calm and relaxed. Should this prove too difficult – the excitement and anticipation is often extremely difficult to contain – it is quite acceptable to suspend the exercise until later, when you have had some time to objectively review what has happened.

Remember, full projection does take time and a lot of practice. However, once it has been confidently and successfully achieved, the boundaries can be extended. Make arrangements to travel astrally to the home of a friend with whom you feel comfortable and who you can trust, someone who lives only a short distance away, and who totally understands exactly what you are endeavouring to achieve. Remember, the experiment must still be carried out in the same way, and the exact same procedure must be followed.

Step Three

- Physically take a casual stroll from your house to your friend's, making a mental note of everything you can see on your journey: the other houses and the way in which they are painted, the gardens and traffic, children playing in the street, people passing by. Take everything in and fix the whole picture in your mind. In other words, mentally record everything so that you can recall it clearly in your imagination later on. If necessary, make the journey several times before beginning the exercise.

- Arrange the co-operation of a friend, and then walk to his or her house and ring the doorbell. Pass through their door, move into their house and into the room where he or she will be sitting during the experiment. When you feel ready, and the exercise has been set up in your mind, follow it in your imagination in exactly the same way as you did with Steps one and Two, going slowly through it stage by stage, until you feel confident that the imagery you have made of yourself is now strong enough to commence the journey to your friend's house.

• Should your attention wander at some point while visualizing yourself making the short journey to your friend's house, imagine yourself walking back to your home, passing through your front door and returning to your chair. Suspend the exercise until later. Never abandon the experiment halfway through, as this merely shows lack of discipline and defeats the whole object of the exercise.

You should be able to see by now that the whole thing is an exercise in mental control, and that by cultivating your powers of visualization you exert a greater control over your mental energies and mobility of consciousness. Once you have successfully gone through the exercise several times, you should be able to relate the things you saw to your friend. Keep a record of how many of the things you experienced could actually be confirmed, as only in this way will you know how successful you have been. Strictly speaking this is not astral projection but remote viewing in preparation for it.

You may initially like to consider not completing the exercise in one sitting. It can be rather laborious and time consuming, and is probably best practised at a time of day or evening when you know you have no other chores and will not be disturbed. The easiest and most effective way is to go through it in stages. Let the first stage be moving to your front door, the second stage as far as the garden gate, the third stage walking a few yards from your house. At the fourth stage, see yourself walking half-way down the street. At the fifth stage, see yourself reaching your friend's front door. At the final stage, enter your friend's home, and see yourself walking into the room where he or she is sitting.

• •

It may all sound fairly straightforward and simple, until you actually attempt to do it. It is not easy to achieve, and a great deal of concentration and patience is required. It may, of course, take you a comparatively short time to achieve full astral projection. It really all depends on your ability to control and project your imagination, and also on the latent potential which you already possess. You may even find yourself projecting spontaneously, without going through the whole procedure of visualization. On the other hand, it may well take you a very long time to achieve. Whichever category you fall into, try not to lose interest, and practise as often as possible, as this is the only way in which results can be positively and successfully achieved.

It may well be that you would simply like to develop or even improve your ability to travel astrally when you sleep. In this case a slightly different approach is needed.

• •

Technique Two
Step One

- First of all, make a note of all your dreams for a full month by keeping a notepad and pen by your bed. Whatever time you retire to bed, set your alarm clock to wake you approximately two and half hours later, at which time you should make a note of anything you can remember dreaming, no matter how vague or ridiculous. Then upon waking in the morning, immediately write down what you experienced when you were asleep. In fact, set your alarm in this way every night for a period of one month, or until you have acquired the habit of waking at this time.

Step Two

- In bed each night, before going to sleep, lie comfortably on your back, preferably with no pillows beneath your head.

- Focus your attention at a chosen spot on the ceiling and stare intently at it without blinking or moving your gaze even for a brief moment.

- Still gazing at the spot on the ceiling, relax your body as completely as you possibly can, and then become conscious of your breathing. As you breathe in feel your abdominal area filling with power and vitality, and on the exhalation feel yourself sinking completely into the bed.

- Allow this slow and rhythmical breathing to continue for several minutes until you are fully relaxed. At this point it is also important that you do not fall asleep, and that you continue to resist the temptation to close your eyes or even to move your gaze away from that spot.

- As you breathe in deeply, feel as though your whole body is being filled with a vitality that gradually makes you feel light, and as you exhale, feel serene and calm. With each inhalation feel your body become almost weightless, and every time you exhale allow yourself to feel more and more at peace. When a state of serenity has been achieved, slowly close your eyes and lie still and calm for a few moments.

- Focus all your energies on your solar plexus, and be totally aware of the rhythm of your breathing.

- Visualize these energies streaming from that area to form a clearly defined, replicated image of yourself, hovering horizontally a few feet above you.

- When you can see this picture clearly in your mind's eye, hold it for a few minutes, then slowly bring it down towards you again, feeling it being drawn once more, as energy into your solar plexus.

- Practise this exercise each night before going to sleep, but still continue to note down all your dreams. Keep a careful record also of anything else you experience when you are asleep.

Step Three

- After a few weeks, when you feel completely confident in your mental imagery of yourself floating above the bed, you should then mentally begin to programme the image of yourself in the following way.

- Concentrate all your energies on the replicated image of yourself, telling it forcefully exactly what you require of it, and what it is that you are trying to achieve. For example: 'I wish to have total control of my dreams, and remember everything about them.'

- Repeat this phrase over and over again, while mentally holding the image of yourself floating above you while you are lying on the bed. In fact, use the phrase as an affirmation with which to programme the image you have created of yourself. By repeating your wishes over and over again, the mental command is gradually taken up by your subconscious mind, and is then passed on to the mental aspects of the astral body.

Practised repeatedly over a period of time, you will be amazed by the results of this exercise. Note how your dream patterns change and become more lucid. Once the desired results have been successfully achieved you may wish to programme not only the way you dream, but the kind of dreams you have, and also improve your memory of them. Simply tell the created image of yourself what to do, such as: 'In my dreams I wish to go to America to visit my cousin, and I wish to have total recall of all that takes place.'

I cannot emphasize enough the importance of the mental repetition of the affirmation, as this infuses the entire exercise with energy and power, and almost lends your astral image wings.

You may of course like to experiment with this technique by making prior arrangements to meet with a friend on the astral plane. Remember, with astral travel distance is unimportant.

• •

Techique Three
Step One

- Tell a trusted friend to spend some time thinking about you just before going to sleep. Arrange to meet in the sleep state at a particular destination such as beneath the town hall clock at, for instance, 3 a.m.

- Having gone through the same procedure of creating the image of yourself floating above you while you are lying on the bed, allow your mind to see the mental image of the town hall clock, making the time on it the time that it really is at that moment.

- Make the image very bright and clear in your mind, and focus your attention on it until five minutes have elapsed on the clock. Your friend should try to imagine you standing under the town hall clock. They should try to hold this picture in their mind for five minutes before going to sleep.

Step Two

- Let your thoughts move away from the picture of the town hall clock and focus your attention on your breathing. Breathe in slowly and deeply, allowing your stomach to rise, and breathe out, watching it fall. Continue this breathing for five minutes, and then gradually allow your mind to drift from your breathing, very slowly creating the clear image of yourself floating above you as you lie on the bed. Make this image very clear and vivid in your mind.

- Once you feel that the picture is strong enough, and you are confident that it is going to work, begin the programming: 'I want to travel to the town hall clock at three o'clock to meet my friend. I want to experience this as strongly and as vividly as though I were there physically, and I wish to recall everything that takes place.'

- Repeat this mental affirmation several times before allowing yourself to fall asleep.

You should keep a careful record of everything that takes place. It may take a few months, or even longer, before anything positive happens. On the other hand, results may be produced in a very short time. It is doubtful, however, that anything other than a pleasant or unusual dream will be experienced on the first night, but practice and determination will eventually produce the desired, successful results.

You should, of course, compare notes with your friend to see if you have been successful in your astral rendezvous. Tell them every detail of the experience, making certain not to miss anything out. Describe where they were standing, what they were doing and exactly what they were wearing, etc.

Remember: you must make sure that the person you will be experimenting with shares the same enthusiasm as yourself, primarily to ensure that he or she really does the experiment, and does not lose interest halfway through. Also, it is a good idea to seek protection before falling asleep, by offering a short, meaningful prayer – in the form of a request for protection from those who are guiding and watching over you in your endeavours.

I should point out that usually the first thing to be developed with such a technique is the ability to programme and remember your dreams. Consequently your dreams will become much more lucid, this being an indication that the astral body is beginning to detach itself more and more under your conscious control.

Here I must sound a cautionary note: should you begin to experience disturbing nightmares it would be wise to leave the techniques alone for a while. This could be an indication that negative forces have somehow found their way into your auric field, in which case your mental energies need to be directed into other things, at least until everything has settled down again. The energy levels do normally recover by themselves, unless of course you are feeling a little run-down physically, or perhaps experiencing a degree of psychological and emotional stress.

If you do have any history of mental illness you would be wise to leave this particular area of the paranormal alone, as it could be detrimental to your overall psychological health.

• •

Chapter Ten

Psychic Healing

No book on psychic development would be complete without some mention of healing, and although many books have been written on this extensive subject, with its many forms and techniques, I would like to explore with you some methods of psychic healing, and offer you some suggestions for the development of such ability.

A psychic healing practitioner is someone who possesses the ability to draw upon large and powerful resources of energy from outside themself, and to transmute and direct that energy for the purpose of restoring the health and vitality of another person's physical body.

This method of healing is not to be confused with *spiritual healing*, which is a completely different concept altogether. The practice of spiritual healing is, in some way, dependent on the belief in a divine, omnipotent power, whilst psychic healing is more to do with the transmutation and control of energy.

I have already defined the nature of prana, and explained that this is the word used in Eastern traditions to describe all energy in the universe. Prana is not only the integrating principle of all things both animate and inanimate, and can be found working through all forms of matter, but it also perpetuates and sustains all life, and when it ceases to be present, death ultimately occurs. Consequently, when the levels of prana are significantly lowered in the physical body for some reason or another, disease manifests in either the body or the mind.

Eastern yogic masters know that by increasing and controlling the incoming streams of prana, they can not only improve their longevity, but also retain their youthfulness, health and vitality. Although it is understood that the fundamental principles underlying the retention of prana in the physical body involve a system of breathing known as *pranayama*, meaning the control of prana, it is further understood by yogic masters that there are some people who quite naturally retain large stores of prana in their bodies. Those who are in their presence for any length of time are suddenly overwhelmed with a sense of invigoration, particularly when they are feeling unwell, run-down or simply under the weather.

The fact that some people appear to possess this potent force in large amounts has nothing whatsoever to do with their anatomical or physiological make-up. I have seen small, slightly built people who were like generators where the psychic force is concerned, and this seems to emit from them rather like powerful surges of electricity. A great many athletes possess strong currents of prana in their bodies, particularly those who work with water, this being a powerful source of prana, and a conduit for the vital force.

Those who work with soil, too, such as farmers or dedicated gardeners, nearly always possess incredible reserves of prana, which very often gives them a serene, calm appearance, which is nearly always transferred to anyone in their presence.

As I have said previously, prana originates from the sun and is stored in the solar plexus, from where it is continually dispensed throughout the body, maintaining balance and health. Normally any depletion of prana in the body is restored through the natural process of breathing, a healthy diet and drinking water. However, in the case of serious illness the depletion of the body's reserves continues until death eventually occurs.

Occasionally the subtle channels in the body along which prana flows become blocked for some reason, thereby preventing a consistent movement of prana. Such blockages produce an effect upon the corresponding parts of the body, thus causing a breakdown in the health of the individual. A visit to either an acupuncturist or reflexologist nearly always alleviates the problem, depending, that is, on the severity of the condition. The acupuncturist will insert fine needles strategically across the patient's body, and after one or two treatments this usually helps to clear the blockages in the subtle channels, thus allowing the prana to flow freely again, thereby alleviating the health problem. Although the same fundamental principles apply to reflexology, with this treatment the belief is that the energy crystallizes where the subtle channels connect in the soles of the feet. The reflexology treatment involves gentle strategic manipulation of the feet, dissipating the crystallized energy and encouraging it to move freely through the channels once again, thereby alleviating the health condition.

You should now have a reasonable understanding of prana and how it can enhance the quality of our lives, so let us now consider the various methods of healing with it.

Technique One

This is a simple experiment to enable you to experience the manifestation of prana in your hands.

- Sit comfortably on a straight-backed chair and place your hands gently on your solar plexus with your eyes closed. Feel the pulse of energy in the abdominal area, and allow your hands to remain in this position for a few moments.

- Now shake your hands vigorously for a minute or so,

allowing your fingers to snap together in the process.

- Whilst your fingers are tingling, with your eyes still closed, place your fingertips gently on your forehead, and feel the vitality passing from your fingers into your head.

- You should now feel a cool, tingling sensation moving across the entire forehead, as prana streams from your fingertips, filling your head completely with vitality.

- Once the tingling has ceased, shake your hands vigorously once again for a few moments, and then repeat the whole process again.

This is a very simple exercise to precipitate the movement of prana in the hands, which can then be conveyed to another part of your body where pain is felt, or even to another person who is unwell. Although prana is very effective in the relief of pain, its effects are not usually permanent. However, when the healing treatment is consistently and frequently administered, it facilitates the self-healing process in any part of the body.

It is not necessary to apply your hands to a specific part of a person's body, as prana creates a powerful circuit in the whole organism, and immediately finds its own level in the body.

• •

As previously said, pranic healing is not, generally speaking, a curative method, but most definitely creates a surge and movement of energy through the body's subtle channels. Once administered to a person who is feeling under the weather, so to speak, the sudden rush has an incredible effect upon the nervous system, thus infusing them with vitality. It does have a powerful effect upon pain and will ease this almost immediately.

The magnetic force of prana is, as I have said elsewhere (see pages 34–6), the fundamental principle underlying most hypnotic treatments. Austrian physician, Franz Anton Mesmer (1734–1815), the innovator of what was termed 'mesmerism', one of the earliest forms of what we know today as hypnotism and which was named after him, made an extensive study of this concept of magnetism and energy.

To effectively produce a hypnotic trance-like state in a patient, the practitioner must understand the concept of energy transference and in theory must learn to project his or her personal magnetism with each intonation of the phrases used in the hypnotic dialogue. Mesmer knew that unless a practitioner of mesmerism was able to project their personal magnetism, the only thing that would transpire between the patient and the practitioner would be a collection of words and phrases.

There is a specific psychology, too, underlying psychic healing, which can be extremely powerful when applied in the correct way. A mother will often rub the winter chill from a child's cold hands saying: 'There you are, now your hands are lovely and warm.' The rubbing motion of the mother's hands not only improves the child's circulation, but through them she also unknowingly imparts streams of prana, which she psychologically enforces with a reassuring statement.

Prana also responds greatly to the imagination, and can be coloured with a specific mission in mind.

. . . .

Technique Two

- Sit your patient on a straight-backed chair and stand behind them. Close your eyes for a few moments and place your hands gently on your patient's shoulders, allowing your thoughts to blend completely with theirs. Once you have attuned yourself to the patient's body, shake your hands vigorously by your sides for a minute or so, and then point both index fingers to the ground, either side of you, imagining streams of energy being drawn up through the extended fingers.

- Still holding your fingers rigid, slowly raise your hands and place one either side of the patient's head, with your index fingers pointing just behind the ears. Breathe in slowly, and as you exhale, mentally discharge the energy from your fingers into the patient's head. Incidentally, there is no need to actually touch the head with your fingers, as it will be more evidential when the force is felt by the patient without physical contact.

- Repeat this process five or six times, always beginning with the vigorous shaking of your hands, thereby stimulating the flow of prana.

- If a patient is suffering from some form of infection and has a high temperature, follow the same procedure, but this time visualize the energy being drawn in and then discharged through your fingertips as being coloured vibrant blue. Should the patient's temperature be low for some reason, simply colour the energy red.

- Conclude the treatment by sweeping your hands up and down the patient's body, either side of them, from the head to the hips, without making physical contact. Then move to the side of the patient and repeat the sweeping process down their front and back.

These cleansing passes of the hands have a stimulating effect on the individual's aura, and also encourage the healing force to circulate more freely throughout the subtle anatomy.

When a person is recovering from illness and is therefore very low in vitality, recovery can be encouraged with the use of a simple treatment I call 'auric and chakra massage'. This treatment not only produces a deep stimulating effect upon the individual's personal energy field, but it also helps to create movement in the channels along which energy is conveyed around the body.

By introducing the appropriate colour into the treatment the person's energy levels may be dramatically increased, causing a sudden rush of vitality, as though the patient had been bathed in a powerful beam of cosmic light.

The healer's ability to visualize is of paramount importance with this treatment, as this will encourage the flow of prana more efficiently.

Technique Three

- For this method of treatment the patient should lie either on the floor or, ideally, on a therapy bed.

- Reassure your patient as much as possible by talking them through relaxation until they feel completely serene and calm. Stand or kneel beside the patient, whichever is appropriate. Place one hand on their forehead, and the other hand on their solar plexus. Remain in this position until you can feel warmth in your hands, and then remove them.

- Now place your left hand over the patient's forehead, without touching it, ideally at a distance of approximately

1 inch (2.5cm) from it. Place your right hand over your left hand, again approximately 1 inch away, without touching it.

- Begin the healing treatment by very slowly moving your left hand in a circular, clockwise motion, and moving your right hand over your left hand, in a circular, anticlockwise motion. Maintain a slow and even movement of your hands, with the fingers on both hands spread apart. Concentrate the movement of both hands over the patient's forehead for at least one minute, longer if you feel necessary. Next, maintaining the rotation of your hands, gradually move them down to the throat area, still not actually touching the patient. Apply the treatment to this spot for a further minute, before moving your hands down to the heart area.

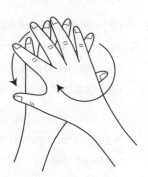

- Remember, the movement of your hands is of paramount importance, to encourage the precipitation of subtle energy in the body.

- Keep the left hand moving slowly with a clockwise motion, and the right hand moving slowly with an anticlockwise motion, ensuring a steady, even rhythm through the entire healing process.

- Now move the rotating hands down to the area just above the naval, remaining there for one minute, longer if you feel necessary.

- Finally, move to the lowest part of the trunk, in the abdominal area, again for one minute.

- The first part of this treatment (as above) should take eight to ten minutes, longer if you feel it is required. The whole treatment should then be repeated, beginning once again with the forehead. However, before you begin again, rest your left hand on the patient's forehead, and your right hand on their solar plexus. Remain in this position as you intuitively determine which colours should be introduced into the next part of the treatment.

- Close your eyes and be intuitively guided to the appropriate colours. Simply flick through the colours of the spectrum in your mind, until one particular colour stands out more than the others. This sounds much more difficult than it actually is, but as your mind processes the colours, simply allow your intuition to make the selection. You will find that this will be done automatically without thought. Once you have concluded the first part of the treatment you should find that you have become closely attuned to your patient, and will just 'know' exactly which colour to use. This colour will more than likely be the one that is lacking in the individual's energy field, and the one that is required to restore balance. You might even find your intuition has selected more than one colour; just be guided by this choice.

- Having intuitively selected the appropriate colour(s), then repeat the healing process with the rotating hands. Begin by moving the left hand in a clockwise motion as before, and the right hand, placed over the left hand without touching it, in an anticlockwise motion. A few seconds into the treatment begin to mentally transmit the chosen colour, by visualizing it being projected from between your brows, passing through your rotating hands, and into the patient. You may feel you need to modify the procedure to

suit you. For example, it might be easier and more
effective for you to simply imagine the colour swirling in
your hands. Do whatever it takes to make the treatment
more effective. If you intuitively selected more than one
colour, simply alternate them during the healing
treatment.

• Remember, it is important that you do not allow your mind
to wander from the imagery during the treatment, as the
lapse in concentration only dissipates the healing rays in
a negative, needless way. You may even find it more
effective when using more than one colour in the healing
process – but at all times be guided by your intuition.

• Work your way slowly down the body, and then ask the
patient to turn over to lie face down, and repeat the process.

• Begin this time with the back of the head, and then
conclude the treatment with the base of the spine. When
the treatment is finished sweep your hands up and down
the patient's body, without touching it, shaking your
hands slightly as you do so. These sweeping passes over
the body produce the effect of sealing the circulating
force, as well as psychologically concluding the whole
treatment. The sweeping passes also have a powerful
cleansing effect upon the individual's aura.

The more you practise this method, the more you may feel
able to do with it. As I have already said, you may even feel
that you need to modify it in some way, perhaps by introducing something else into the healing process. This really does
not matter, as long as the motions of the hands, moving in
opposite directions, are maintained in the treatment. If your
coordination is not good, you may even have to practise

rotating your hands in this way before you actually administer healing to a person.

This treatment is very effective on those with respiratory conditions or digestive problems, and in the easing of debilitating spinal conditions. The process also affects the individual chakras and encourages the correct polarity to be restored in each one.

● ●

Remember, should you lack confidence in your skills as a psychic healer, this will transfer to the person you are treating and then ultimately interfere with the whole healing process. It might be a good idea before embarking upon the path of healing to practise for a while on a family member or friend. If you have no confidence in what you are doing, then the person you are treating will have no confidence in it either. So be certain that you *know* you do have the power within you to heal. Have faith and confidence, and then the power will be much more effective.

Administering psychic healing on a regular basis, allowing yourself little or no time to recover your own energies, will very quickly send you into poor health. Once your levels of vitality have been allowed to fall below a certain degree, you may have extreme difficulty in raising them again. So you must safeguard against the depletion of your own vitality by allowing yourself some time to recover between healing treatments. Tiredness is one of the primary symptoms of depletion in the vital force, as are irritability and nervousness. Should you allow this state to persist, you will most certainly find yourself becoming more susceptible to minor illnesses, infections and nervous disorders. This warning applies to any form of psychic work, regardless of how strong and healthy the practitioner actually is.

Take time away from your healing work. Take long walks in the park or countryside, and enjoy plenty of fresh air. Eat lots of fruit and fresh green vegetables, and try to drink at least two pints of water charged with prana each day. Charge your water in the way I have previously mentioned, pouring it from one vessel to another, passing it backwards and forwards, over and over, through the air, until it has the appearance of being almost alive with vitality. When drinking the charged water hold it in your mouth for a few moments, washing it around the tongue to absorb the prana, before eventually swallowing it.

In the early stages of your development, rest as much as possible, particularly before administering healing treatment. Try to retire to bed as early as possible, especially the night before a busy healing day.

The most effective exercise for replenishing the nervous system with vitality is one I frequently use, primarily to 'recharge my batteries'.

• •

Exercise 29

- Sit in an erect posture with your back straight, and place your fingertips gently on your solar plexus. Breathe in very slowly, imagining streams of prana as intense vibrant white light, passing through your nostrils and down into your lungs, then into your solar plexus, where they are immediately taken up by your fingertips.

- When your breath is complete, hold it for a few moments, whilst slowly transferring your fingertips, containing the white light, gently to your forehead. Exhale very slowly, mentally watching the intense white light streaming from your fingertips, filling your head completely.

- Once again, when you have fully expelled all the air from your lungs, hold your breath once again, whilst returning your fingertips to your solar plexus, repeating the whole process.

- Breathe in very slowly, mentally watching streams of intense white light moving through your nostrils, down into your lungs, and then into your solar plexus. When the breath is complete, hold it whilst transferring the white light in your fingertips once again to your forehead. Breathe the white light through your fingertips, filling your head completely with vitality.

Repeat the exercise several times, longer if necessary, until you experience a tingling sensation in your hands, or on your forehead, or even both.

Once again I must stress the importance of the imagery here, as it is this that adds force to the effectiveness of the exercise. You should not allow your mind to wander from the visualization even for a moment, as this would merely defeat the whole object of the exercise, which is to restore vitality to the nervous system and replenish the depleted levels of pranic energy in the subtle channels of your body.

Mastering the technique of accumulating great stores of prana in the body is something that develops gradually over a period of time, once you have come to know exactly what this energy is, and have truly begun to use it in your healing treatments.

Of course, as I have already explained, the body's inpouring streams of prana may be encouraged by the use of specific breathing methods and visualization techniques. Once this has been achieved, streams of prana may easily be directed towards a sick person, accompanied by a specific mental command, in order to encourage the healing process.

This method calls for a great deal of concentration, and confidence in one's healing skills, but once it has been administered correctly, positive results are nearly always achieved almost immediately.

Exercise 30

- Before administering healing, sit comfortably once again on a straight-backed chair, with your mind totally focused on yourself and the powers you possess within. Breathe rhythmically for a few minutes, paying particular attention to your inhalations and the incoming force. Allow your diaphragm to expand as you breathe in slowly and deeply, and feel invigorated as your body absorbs the inpouring prana, before breathing out slowly.

- Extend your arms at 45 degrees, with the palms of your hands facing inwards, and on the slow inhalation of breath, draw them slowly inwards and place the palms of your hands flat against your chest. Exhale fully.

- Extend your arms once again, the palms of your hands facing inwards, and repeat the whole process again. In fact, repeat the exercise five or six times, simply following the slow rhythm of your breathing, and then gradually begin to introduce specific revitalizing colours to infuse the inflowing prana. This time, when you inhale, imagine streams of pink energy flowing into your body. Watch it carefully, passing through your nostrils and down into your lungs. When you exhale, see all the waste and toxins pouring out from you. Give these a murky green or grey colour.

• Continue the exercise for a further five to eight minutes and then relax.

Remember not to make these exercises a labour, as that would again defeat the whole object of the exercise, and would deplete your energy levels rather than increase them.

● ●

You should feel fully 'charged' after this exercise, and ready to commence with the healing treatment. It is not enough to simply administer healing to a patient without first reassuring them. Before beginning, first explain to them what it is you are trying to achieve, and DO NOT make the healing process seem mysterious, as this would make the person you are treating tense or even anxious. It is important to interact with the patient, accompanying your treatment with a verbal explanation about what you are doing and what exactly he or she must expect. Should the individual feel a little uncomfortable with you, the process of healing will be restricted as a consequence of the mental barrier which they will have created as a form of defence.

Nor should you begin the treatment as soon as the patient enters the room. Take time to exchange a few pleasantries and general conversation, and try not to be too clinical in your approach, as this can also be a little off-putting to many people. Remember, too, that you are not medically qualified (even if you are) so never offer a diagnosis regardless of how psychically or intuitively impressed you are during the treatment. Apart from anything else, diagnosing illness, or even suggesting what medication should be taken or not taken, whichever the case may be, is illegal and so should be avoided at all times. Today the law is quite strict where psychics and alternative practitioners are concerned, so one should always work to a strict moral code of practice.

It is important to rest for a time before the healing treatment begins, particularly in cases where the patient is suffering from serious illness. It is also advisable to eat sparingly before administering healing, as this too may cause you adverse effects.

As with all psychic work, prepare yourself mentally for the patient, creating 'mind pictures' of the health condition you wish to achieve.

The following treatment may be applied to most health conditions, but it may be particularly effective in the easing of pain, especially where the lungs and stomach areas are involved.

• •

Technique Four
Step One

Ask the patient to lie on their stomach, preferably on a treatment bed. Standing alongside the patient, with your eyes closed, move your hands fairly quickly across and up and down the body, at a distance of approximately 2–3in (5–8cm) from it, without actually touching. Mentally 'scan' the patient's body in this way until you feel intuitively guided to a specific part of their anatomy, and then simply hold your hands steadily over that point.

• At first, do not think of anything in particular, but simply allow your hands to remain in that position. The patient's body will draw the prana it needs from your hands – and you may soon feel that they are becoming quite warm.

- At this point, focus all your energies into your hands, sending the mental command to the patient's body: 'Pain be released! Pain be released!'

- Repeat this mentally, over and over again, until you feel impressed to move on. Continue to mentally scan the body with your hands, allowing your intuition to guide you to where the healing is needed. Although it is not essential for you to close your eyes, you may find that your intuition works more efficiently when external distractions are eliminated.

- This may sound fanciful and far-fetched to some people, but believe me, it is an extremely effective method, and one that can create a great deal of energy which is then discharged into the patient.

- Once you feel that the 'scanning' process has been fully exhausted, move on to the next step.

Step Two

- Still standing alongside the patient, shake your hands vigorously by your sides until they feel 'alive' with energy. While your hands are still tingling place them gently on the back of the patient's head. Hold your hands in that position until the tingling has ceased, and then withdraw them from the patient's head.

- Shake your hands vigorously once again for a full minute. This time, place your left hand on the left side of the patient's back, around the lung area, and your right hand on the right side of their back. Hold your hands in that position until the tingling in them has ceased.

- Next, make sweeping passes up and down the spine, from the base of the skull to the base of the spine, imagining the patient bathed in the colour green. Mentally infuse this colour with a force that becomes more potent with each exhalation of your breath.

- Continue this for as long as you feel necessary, and then ask the patient to turn onto their back.

- Repeat the process, allowing your hands to be intuitively guided.

The same procedure should be followed each time, regardless of whether or not you already know what is wrong with the patient. Where psychic healing is concerned treatment should be applied to the *whole* person, as opposed to just the affected part of the body. However, particular attention may be concentrated on the troubled part of the person's anatomy, just to encourage the healing process a little more effectively.

• •

The head, the lungs, the spine and the stomach play an extremely important part in the assimilation and transmutation of subtle energy. By encouraging the movement of the force in these anatomical areas, balance may easily be restored to the body's natural processes. Particular attention should always be paid to the stomach area, as this is usually where most of the person's energy reserves are stored, and a depletion in energy levels is usually first to occur in this area. Therefore, by concentrating the healing at this point (stomach), and accompanying it with a specific revitalizing colour, such as orange, the energy levels may be increased, and the healing process encouraged.

Transmitting colour mentally means that the shade and intensity can be altered immediately, and combinations of colours can be introduced instantly, without the patient even realizing what has happened.

Experimentation is important when working with colour, and a process of elimination should be applied when treating certain illnesses with colour energy. You may even find that the way you work in the field of psychic healing is unique to you; as long as you achieve positive results, it really does not matter.

The following short table of colours may be of some help to you initially. To give you some guidance I have listed various colours alongside the conditions that usually respond to them.

Red Lethargy; blood disorders; lack of appetite; poor circulation.

Blue Painful and inflammatory conditions affecting any part of the body; psychological problems, such as anxiety, depression. Promotes general toning and calming of the nerves.

Yellow Liver conditions; kidneys and bowels; some lung conditions where energy is required. Has the effect of stimulating the major organs.

Green Heart; lungs; low body weight; run-down; eye problems; nervous disorders. Promotes balance in body, mind and spirit.

Orange Lack of energy; loss of appetite and vitality; pneumonia; some stomach conditions; irritable bowel syndrome.

Violet A powerful energy which produces holistic results. A good all-round healing colour. Promotes balance in the

body and the mind; calms the nervous system and aids
general recovery from illness.

Combinations of colours may be used when mentally transmitting.
You would obviously have great difficulty imagining two colours
simultaneously, but, by alternating their mental transmission, they
can form an extremely powerful force in the treatment of some
health conditions. The mental transmission of colours for the
purpose of healing should not be underestimated. It is an excellent
way of directing currents of prana with the intention of facilitating
the healing force. Red combined with green, for example, is
effective in the treatment of jaundice, and bright red combined
with orange is very effective in the treatment of exhaustion.

Remember, your powers of visualization are important in this
form of psychic therapy treatment, as is your ability to concentrate
all your powers into one specific area.

The use of colour in healing has, in fact, been used for
thousands of years, and its effectiveness on disease has been
explored by many ancient cultures. The results of this sort of
therapy are dependent upon your powers of visualization,
combined with the belief that you *do* possess a powerful force
within you that can heal and in many cases cure disease.

Chapter Eleven

Meditation: Key to Self-Mastery

When I speak of meditation, I am talking about a specific system of mental exercises designed primarily to cultivate awareness with the sole object of precipitating the consciousness. Occasionally meditation is able to transcend consciousness, and is in fact the means by which all great minds aspire to cultivate a greater awareness of the soul and its independence of the body. Apart from this, though, meditation is the key to self-mastery and a prerequisite when one is creating a psychic development programme.

As this book is primarily about developing your psychic powers, we will confine ourselves to those techniques of meditation that will encourage concentration and aid the cultivation of these faculties.

Although group meditation can be extremely effective when one is seeking to attain a higher level of consciousness and develop psychic abilities, it is my belief that not all methods of meditation are suitable for some people, who may also feel uncomfortable when meditating in a group. The effects of meditation certainly vary from person to person, and what technique suits one individual may not suit another. A meditation technique may be specifically designed to suit the individual, as not all people find it easy to make the mind quiet and focus their attention for any length of time. Also, some people find it difficult to hold an abstract thought in the mind for a single moment, let alone for ten minutes, and may find it easier to gaze at a geometric shape, which requires very little effort at all.

Before a meditation routine is created, the whole psychology of the individual must first be considered, primarily to ensure that the exercises used are going to be effective, and are not going to be abandoned as a waste of time.

Although generally speaking, any mental exercise that controls the thought processes may be considered to be meditation, the individual should look upon it as a joyful procedure rather than a labour, which would simply defeat the whole object of the exercise, which is to focus the attention on one specific point.

You can be quite certain that as long as the correct technique of meditation is used, the benefits will be experienced at all levels of the user's existence, and will even in the long term affect some profound changes in the individual's outlook on life itself. There is very little doubt that when meditation is integrated into one's daily routine, the health as well as the whole psychology of the individual greatly improves.

The three-fold-attunement meditation approach is one technique which most people find of great benefit when endeavouring to cultivate the senses. It is a technique that encapsulates the whole person, bringing together the emotional, mental and spiritual aspects of one's nature. It involves the three steps: *Contemplation*, *Concentration* and finally *Meditation*.

• •

Exercise 31

- Sit on a straight-backed chair, and begin as always with some rhythmic breathing, so as to slow everything down and reduce the level of activity in the mind.

- Check that your posture is comfortable, and that your back is straight with your shoulders thrown slightly back, and your hands are resting lightly in your lap.

Step One: Contemplation

- Focus your thoughts on your reason for meditating, asking yourself what it is you are trying to achieve, but at the same time trying not to make your reason too complicated.

- Having decided exactly what it is, establish it fully in your mind, and for five minutes or more contemplate its possibilities. Doing this establishes your connections with the universe and mentally releases your intentions. In fact, for a few minutes contemplate your relationship with the universe.

- In your contemplative state look at yourself objectively and try to see yourself as others see you. Perhaps here you can use the same imagery process as you did in the astral projection exercise in Chapter Nine. Should the image you have of yourself appear weak and lacking in confidence, make an asserted effort to change this image into someone who is strong, confident, and even dynamic. Spend some time on this until you can see yourself clearly.

- The period of contemplation is used to prepare the mind for the next phase, that of concentration. Concentrating for any length of time can be extremely tiring, but a few moments spent in contemplation gently prepare the mind and place it into the correct mental frame, making concentration much easier.

Step Two: Concentration

- With your eyes open, focus your gaze on a point of space in front of you, as always resisting the temptation to move your eyes or blink. When your eyes begin to water and you can no longer gaze, allow your eyes to slowly close.

- At this point you should focus your attention on the top of your head. Allow your attention to penetrate the crown of your skull, imagining a small violet, spiralling light at that point. See it glowing brightly and swirling with a clockwise motion.

- Allow your focus to move through the swirling violet light, down to the space just between your brows, and now become aware of a pulsating point of deep blue light. Allow this to hold your attention for a few moments, and then gradually move your attention inwardly toward the throat area. Here you become conscious of a bright blue coruscating radiation of light that seems almost transcendental in appearance. Focus on this for a few moments.

- Next, allow your attention to pass inwardly to the region of the heart. Allow yourself to be overwhelmed by a beautiful shade of aquamarine that quivers and appears translucent and almost unreal. Feel this colour quickening your senses and sending a surge of energy all through your body. In fact, experience this colour at an emotional level, before eventually moving your focus to the area just below the left side of your ribcage, where you become conscious of a sparkling deep yellow, swirling light. Focus your attention on this for a few moments and be aware of it expanding as you watch it move with a clockwise motion. Focus on it for a few moments longer, mentally drinking in the vibrant stimulation of the yellow.

- Move your attention to the naval area and become aware of an intense orange light, giving you a feeling of strength and clarity of thought. Allow your attention to be drawn inwardly to this point and to be overwhelmed by its sheer strength and vitality. Remain here for a few moments, imbibing its immense power.

- Move your awareness to the base of your spine, where you feel your consciousness drawn into a fiery glow. Feel the spontaneous energy as your consciousness is drawn deeper into a red, fiery whirlpool, from which you are conscious of streams of vitality moving up your spine to the crown of your head.

- Spend a few minutes allowing your attention to move backwards and forwards over all these beautiful colours, exploring each one individually, before seeing them collectively manifest as one huge kaleidoscopic mass swirling inside and about you. See all the colours pouring from you into one swirling pool of energy in front of you.

- Imagine now that the swirling pool of colour has suddenly transmuted into a pond of intense blue water, across the surface of which the sunlight is reflected.

- Now you can see a setting sun, rather like a huge ball of fire in the sky, reflected across the surface of the pond, filling you with an overwhelming sense of peace and serenity. Imbibe the solar energy and allow it to fill your very being.

- Allow your attention to be drawn down through the surface of the water, and now feel yourself surrounded once again by swirling colours. Feel as though a powerful transcendental force has filled your whole body, and that you and the swirling colours have suddenly become as one.

- Hold this experience for five or ten minutes, allowing your mind to create its own imagery. Go with it, whatever you see, and then, when you feel ready, dissolve the whole meditation from your mind.

As well as the intended results, the exercises in contemplation and concentration encourage the image-making faculty to develop. It is important to read through the instructions a few times, primarily to ensure that you do not need to keep checking them and can follow the exercises with great ease.

Step Three: Meditation

- Mentally, see yourself sitting at the bottom of a pool of crystal clear water, able to breathe and to see flashes of colour produced by the setting sun above you. Allow your attention to focus on a white lotus flower in front of you, lying on the bed of the pool.

- Mentally pick up the lotus flower in cupped hands and see yourself holding it upwards, your arms outstretched to the cascading light.

- Allow yourself mentally to rise to your feet, and see yourself floating to the surface of the pond, still clutching the beautiful white lotus flower. Mentally allow yourself to emerge through the surface of the pool, into the beautiful light produced by the setting sun, burning like a huge ball of fire on the horizon. Once again, imbibe the powerful solar energies, allowing them to fill your whole body. Hold the lotus flower up to the fiery sky which is awash with purple, green, red, yellow and orange flames.

- Hold the lotus flower close to your breast, and then with outstretched arms, proffer it to the sun, and watch as the lotus metamorphoses into a beautiful butterfly that moves gracefully away on the gentle breeze. See its gossamer-like wings, iridescent in the glowing sunlight, and watch as it moves away into nothingness.

- Sit for a few moments replaying the imagery in your mind and then gently open your eyes.

This particular meditation is an exercise in colour. As well as having a profound effect upon the senses, it also helps to encourage more clarity in the colours of the aura, making them sharper and much more intense. The exercise also has a psychological effect by encouraging a more balanced relationship between body and mind.

● ●

Through meditation, the mind is able to exert greater control of the subtle energies of the aura, and will encourage these to radiate and to move more freely through the channels of vitality.

Activating and releasing the inherent qualities of the individual chakras may be achieved with various mental techniques, but their activation can be initiated with a method of mental activity specifically designed for such a purpose.

Each chakra is represented symbolically by a geometric shape called a *yantra*, which externally represents the inherent qualities of the centre to which it corresponds, primarily for the purpose of meditation. These yantras may be used alone, or combined with a powerful word that represents the chakra, called a *bija-mantra*. Yantras and bija-mantras are used together in a system of meditation primarily to create activity in their corresponding chakras, thereby encouraging the release of their full creative and psychic potential. Once the activity has been created in the individual chakras, the energies produced can then be released through a further process of meditation. As very little effort is required for this method of meditation, the majority of people find it quite easy to follow.

Before going any further, let us look at the chakras and their corresponding yantras and bija-mantras.

It is obviously a good idea to write the bija-mantras down on separate cards, and then learn them by rote. Fixing them in your memory will allow you to use them with much greater ease and confidence – so important to the process of chanting. The yantras are easy to make; as long as the shapes and individual colours are more or less correct, what you make them from is not that important. However, the most effective way is to make them from pieces of card, simply by copying the shapes illustrated opposite.

Try to use, if possible, a translucent, brightly coloured paint or card colour, as this will facilitate the mental imagery as the shapes are processed in the mind, thus encouraging concentration.

Exercise 32

Although bija-mantras may be used individually, or combined with their corresponding yantras, the simplest and most effective way to use them is to chant the bija-mantras sequentially, backwards and forwards, until the energy has been sufficiently created. This particular method does not include the yantras, as these may be introduced into the exercise later, perhaps when you have mastered the technique of chanting more fully.

Bija-Mantra	Yantra	Corresponding Chakra
Lam		Muladhara (base of spine)
Vam		Svadisthana (navel)
Ram		Manipura (solar plexus)
Yam		Anahata (heart)
Ham		Vishudda (throat)
Ksham		Ajna (brow)
Om		Sahasrara (crown)

- First of all acquaint yourself with the bija-mantras so that you can chant them without hesitation. Although you have written them down, it is a good idea to learn them by rote, to ensure that you can chant with your eyes closed, and that a consistent rhythm is maintained throughout the chanting process.

- Sit in a comfortable position on a straight-backed chair, with your shoulders thrown slightly back, and your hands resting lightly on your lap.

- The chanting should be carried out in the following way: Slowly inhale a complete breath, filling your lungs with air, and then on the exhalation commence chanting, breathing in again when appropriate. You will need to establish your own pace to maintain a steady rhythm.

- The bija-mantras should be chanted in quick succession, beginning with 'Lam' and concluding with 'Om'.

- Repeat the process of chanting the bija-mantras, over and over again, until you feel your head and body are almost 'buzzing'.

- At this point, begin to clap your hands vigorously in unison with each intonation. Continue chanting and clapping your hands for a further five minutes, longer if possible, then suspend the whole process, close your eyes (if open), and then rest your hands gently on your solar plexus. You should now feel the vibration in your hands and through your entire body.

- Now, imagine the energy moving through the individual chakras, as though passing up from the earth, through the base chakra, working its way upwards, touching each chakra en route to the crown of the head.

- When the vibration has ceased, resume the chanting for a further five minutes, and then accompany it with clapping.

- With your eyes still closed, see the energy moving through the chakras, drawing to itself their inherent colours as it passes from one to the other. Allow the energy to move freely through the channels, maintaining a steady, consistent flow. Should it appear restricted in any way, mentally encourage it on its way.

- Repeat this process for 20 minutes, longer if you wish. The longer you do it the more invigorating it will feel and the more power will be created.

This exercise is invigorating and has a tendency to stimulate the energy levels of the practitioner. Over a period of time it will heighten the awareness and make the psychic faculties much more responsive. It will also help to balance the individual chakras by creating in each the correct movement of energy. Although the chanting process is extremely effective when practised alone, the chanting of a group is far more audibly exciting.

Exercise 33

With this exercise I would suggest that you work on one chakra a day, completing the entire system in one week. I would also suggest that it only be practised for one month out of three, to allow the results to fully take effect. Work your way up through the chakras, from muladhara to sahasrara, changing the corresponding yantra and bija-mantra, on consecutive days.

- Place the first yantra (yellow square) facing you at eye level. Gaze at the centre of it without blinking or moving your gaze away. Stare at it until you can no longer look without blinking to clear your eyes.

- Close your eyes and place the palms of your hands over them, applying a slight pressure to your eyeball.

- As soon as the after-image of the yantra appears in the mind's eye, commence chanting the corresponding bija-mantra by inhaling a full and complete breath, and on the exhalation sound the word 'Lam' loudly and deeply. Close your lips at the end of the word and allow the 'm' sound to fill the air and vibrate at the back of your nasal passages, until the breath has been fully expelled. The resonation from your chanting should be felt deep within the area of the chakra.

- Inhale a deep breath immediately, and repeat the chanting, and then continue until the after-image has dissolved completely.

- Suspend the chanting, open your eyes and return your gaze to the yantra, and repeat the whole process.

- Continue this exercise for as long as it feels comfortable, remembering not to strain it in anyway whatsoever.

Remember not to make the chanting laborious, as this will defeat the object of the exercise, which is of course to produce a calming, rhythmical effect upon the mind, and also to introduce activity into the corresponding chakra.

• •

In the Western world the majority of people tend to be emotionally inhibited, and are very often enslaved by their emotions. But India, for example, does not appear to have the same problem, its people being very much in control of their insidious emotions. Meditation is very often an integral part of the educational curriculum in India, and today it is taught in many countries to very young children.

Children who have been taught some form of meditation nearly always have less aggressive natures, and are often much more sensitive than those who have not been introduced to it. This would substantiate the claims made by many notable meditation teachers and their devotees that meditation alleviates stress by lowering blood pressure, thereby lessening the risk of heart disease.

However, there are many more benefits because, when practised regularly over a period of time, meditation can certainly heighten one's awareness and also aid the cultivation of the creative and intuitive faculties. Meditation enhances the quality of one's life and is capable of promoting longevity. In fact, in the 1960s, at the height of the so-called Flower Power era, the Maharishi Mahesh Yogi, a physicist, developed a system of meditation he called 'Transcendental Meditation'. This method of producing altered states of consciousness was based on a yogic system of meditation, similar to the method given above, involving a mantra. The Maharishi claimed that each student of his meditation was given an individual personal mantra. Although those practising Transcendental Meditation are told not to use any mental force, it is my belief that the word itself is not of any great importance and that any word will suffice as a mantra, as long as the meditator feels comfortable using it. However, this is a matter of opinion, as all meditation techniques can be modified and tailored to suit the individual.

Transcendental Meditation itself is a modified version of some forms of yoga meditation in which the eyes should be closed and the attention turned inwards. When the mind wanders, the mantra should then be reintroduced, encouraging the attention to be focused once again. The use of a mantra is extremely effective in controlling the mind and making it more focused. This sort of discipline is a prerequisite when endeavouring to cultivate the psychic faculties. Incidentally, a cross-legged posture is not necessary when practising meditation, unless you find it more comfortable that is. Sitting on a straight-backed chair in the Egyptian posture is most probably more suitable for the Western anatomy, back straight, feet on the floor, head tilted slightly back. Anyway, unless you are devotee of yoga, the lotus or cross-legged posture will probably be uncomfortable for you.

A mantra does not have to be a single word, it can be a whole phrase or even a sequence of words meaningful to you. One which I find most effective, both as a mantra and as a means of encouraging the development of the creative and psychic faculties, is the well-known *Om Mani Padme Hum* literally meaning 'Om, The Jewel in the Lotus'. This can be repeated mentally, while visualizing a beautiful lotus flower containing within its petals a glistening, multifaceted diamond, or some other precious gemstone. However, initially you will probably find this exercise quite difficult to achieve, so I would suggest using the mantra by itself at first.

Although it is nearly always suggested that *Om Mani Padme Hum* be repeated mentally, I find that bringing it *audibly* to the lips helps to cultivate correct breath control, as well as producing some amazing vibrations in the surrounding atmosphere.

Simply inhale a complete breath and commence chanting the sequence of words over and over again, ensuring that the rhythm of the sounds is even and consistent. I believe it is more effective initially if the phrase is chanted at least three times in succession before pausing for breath, but always remember not to strain or make it a labour. Should you feel it is simply not practical to audibly produce the mantra, repeat it mentally, not permitting any space to form between each word, so that one runs into the next with a steady rhythm. The lips and tongue should remain still, and the mind focused totally on the repetition of the phrase.

Exercise 34

- Focus your attention on the screen of your mind, and create a very still pond. See a light reflected across the surface of the pond, and even see you own reflection in the water. In the centre of the pond create a beautiful lotus flower, and see a small jewel in the centre of it. Make no attempt to mentally touch the jewel, but focus your attention totally on it. Be conscious of your breathing, ensuring that it is slow and even.

- Mentally make a detailed analysis of the jewel in the lotus flower, exploring its hidden qualities. Examine the flower's perfume and the texture of its petals. Mentally touch the jewel with your fingers and feel its coolness and smoothness. See how the sunlight catches each facet, breaking up into a myriad of colours and shades, and allow your imagination total freedom.

- Hold the picture of the jewel and the lotus flower steadily in the mind and absorb the stillness, the peace and the total serenity.

- Once you have a clear picture fully established in your imagination, it may be a good idea to introduce the mantra *Om Mani Padme Hum*. Repeat it over and over again while you hold the picture firmly and steadily in your mind.

As with other techniques, this exercise may be modified and

changed in a way that suits your ability to focus and concentrate. The mantra and the visualization can be used independently of each other. Either way, the lotus flower exercise will serve as a useful method of developing one's sensitivity and awareness.

• •

It is easy to be put off by complex terminology and systems of meditation, but many people find that the most simplistic methods are also the most effective. It is important to experiment with as many techniques as possible until you find the method that suits you, and which is compatible with your capabilities.

Meditation is often productive of symbols, which can themselves be used as focal points for meditation. The following experiment in creative visualization is one such method, and one that most people enjoy and find quite easy to follow.

• •

Exercise 35

- Imagine yourself standing on the bank of a very large lake. The water is still and very clear in front of you. On the other side of the lake there are some mountains. The sky is very blue and clear, the sun is shining full and bright and is reflected across the surface of the lake.

- As you stand at the edge of the lake, feel the gentle breeze against your face. Listen to the birds whistling and singing unseen from the trees around you. Hear the monotonous drone of a bumble bee as it settles on a flower beside you. Drink in the peace and serenity of the whole picturesque landscape.

- As you gaze thoughtfully out across the lake, you notice a staircase emerging from the water, extending far up into the blueness of the sky above. Allow your attention to focus on the staircase, and then suddenly feel yourself moving across the surface of the lake, without touching the water, until you come to rest at the foot of the staircase.

- Begin to climb the stairs, one step at a time, and as you ascend, see the water below you still and calm. Move your eyes to the hills and mountains on the other side of the lake, and then to the blue sky and warm sun. Feel yourself passing through the blue of the sky until you are completely surrounded by it.

- Reach the top of the staircase and pause for a moment to look around you. Feel yourself bathed in the cool and relaxing vibrations of blue. As you glance to the side you notice a small casket appear, as if by magic, floating in the air. Mentally will the casket to move towards you and pick it up. Hold it close to you and pull back the lid. Retrieve whatever is inside – let it be the first thing that comes into your mind. Do not change it, even if you find the object unpleasing.

- You notice a piece of parchment and a pen also in the casket. Write a single word on the parchment and then return it to the casket, along with the pen and your object. Close the lid, and then watch as the casket moves away from you, eventually disappearing into nothingness.

- Begin to slowly descend the staircase, allowing your eyes to move about you all the time, watching the blue of the sky now above you, and the lake below you moving nearer. See the hills and the mountains, the sky and the bright sun.

- Reach the foot of the staircase and feel yourself gliding across the surface of the water, until you finally settle once again on the grassy bank. Stand for a moment imbibing the peace and stillness; the birds singing in the trees, the gentle hypnotic rustling of the leaves.

- Allow your attention to move to the centre of the lake and see the staircase slowly disappearing into the still water. Once it has gone completely, leaving slight ripples on the surface of the water, breathe in slowly and deeply, and when you breathe out allow the picture to dissolve completely from your mind, then relax for a few moments.

In this exercise you projected your consciousness into the imagery of the meditation, and experienced colour, sound and form.

Your ascent of the staircase symbolized the raising of the level of your awareness. At the top of the staircase you allowed yourself to interact with the blue of the sky and the casket. You used all your senses and became totally involved with the imagery.

Whatever you retrieved from the casket more than likely possesses symbolic meaning, and represents something of deep, spiritual significance. As the object was produced by your own subconscious, only you possess the power to interpret its true meaning. Take your object with you into a future meditation and use it as a focal point of contemplation. The answer to its meaning will come to you in the quietness.

While in the quietness, contemplate upon whatever you wrote on the piece of parchment. The next time you ascend the staircase in your meditation see if the word you wrote has changed.

• •

Meditation is the means by which all great minds aspire to higher levels of consciousness, in an asserted effort to attain a state of *nirvana*. The state of nirvana transcends words and even consciousness and can only be expressed by *being*. As long as the technique works for you, and produces positive results for you, which meditation you use is not that important.

It must also be borne in mind that whatever method of meditation you do use, it is best practised at a time of day when you are not tired and therefore not in danger of falling asleep, and also at a time when you know you will not be disturbed. It should be practised on an empty stomach, either before you eat or at least one hour after.

I always find it of great benefit to use the same room each time I meditate. If possible, create a small sanctuary for yourself, or if practical (weather permitting), use a quiet corner of the garden. It also helps to create the right atmosphere if you burn some pleasant incense. Dedication is also vitally important where meditation is concerned. Try to practise your meditation consistently, at more or less the same time every day.

Never force meditation, and always look upon it as one endless experiment. Should you ever have a sense of having achieved something in meditation, then you have more than likely achieved nothing at all. Try not to approach your meditation with any one particular aim in mind, for the achievement is in the actual practice of it. Therefore, although it is the object of this book to aid you in the development of your psychic powers, do not practise meditation with this specifically in mind. Make meditation an integral part of your daily routine and expect nothing from it, and you should then achieve everything.

Finally, although meditation is the key to self-mastery, and also the means with which to cultivate the senses and heighten the awareness, by itself it will not develop your psychic abilities. Meditation is one of many tools in the toolbox of the master craftsman. You are that craftsman, and you already possess psychic skills potentially. It is hoped that this book will help you to cultivate and hone those skills until they have been sufficiently sharpened for you to use.

Chapter Twelve

Miscellaneous

Psychic Handwriting Analysis

There are innumerable ways of gleaning information about the future. Once your psychic powers have been fully established, you will become a conduit for the psychic force, and may sometimes find information about a person just 'popping' into your mind. Once you have cultivated the faculties and refined your sensitivity, you should prepare yourself for all eventualities. You are a unit of incredible power; an electromagnetic force that is capable of pulling energy from everything around you.

Some years ago I found I had an aptitude for psychically picking things up from people's handwriting. I would simply briefly scan a sample of handwriting to glean all sorts of information about the individual who had written it. I developed this method of divination into a fine art, and today I receive letters from all over the world requesting a *psychic handwriting analysis*.

Psychic handwriting analysis is completely different from graphology, which itself is a precise science, and involves an extensive and meticulous study of the structure and formation of the writing. Whilst the information obtained by means of graphology is fairly extensive, it is confined to the writer's general character, skills and mood tendencies, and also some health problems, but it certainly cannot reveal information pertaining to the individual's future.

Psychic handwriting analysis is a completely different concept because the information is gleaned through psychic means, and therefore the past, the present and the future become apparent to me, simply by scanning the handwriting, or even holding it gently in my fingertips without looking at it. I suppose one could say that it is a form of psychometry that works by looking at it as well as by touch.

Over the years I have found that some handwriting 'speaks' very clearly and loudly, and appears to want to tell all about the writer, while other handwriting appears shy and afraid, and almost reluctant to reveal information. This is the only way I am able to describe the process of psychic handwriting analysis, because the information gleaned from it varies from person to person.

While this method of divination cannot really be taught, I can offer you some pointers and general guidelines as to how you can make psychic handwriting analysis work for you.

• •

Exercise 36

- Working with a group, ask everyone to obtain some samples of handwriting from people they know quite well. This will allow any information given during the exercise to be confirmed.

- Distribute the handwriting samples to the group, ensuring that each person receives a sample of writing unknown to them.

- Sit quietly with the sample of handwriting, and allow your eyes to scan it continuously backwards and forwards. Impressions might come to you almost immediately, and as you did with the psychometry exercise, write these down straight away.

- First, get a general feeling for the writer's character and emotional status. Are they happy? Are they alone in life? What sort of career if any do they have? Does the handwriting represent a creative person? In fact, resist the temptation to make a detailed analysis of the style of writing, and just allow your imagination to create its own pictures.

- It is important to constantly ask yourself questions, jotting down the answers immediately. In fact, it is always important to respond to the first thing that comes into your mind. A lot of the information should come voluntarily, but the rest will require some persuasion.

- Use all your senses during the analysis; smell the writing, feel it, listen to it and allow your eyes to constantly move across it. In other words, become totally involved with the writing, allowing your mind to blend completely with it.

- Obviously, check the accuracy of the information you have gleaned once you have completed the exercise.

• •

It may well be that the process of psychic handwriting analysis is not your forte, and therefore will not work for you. Some people's sensitivity simply does not work along certain lines, and their particular skills may need a different expression. Although it is a psychic ability, psychic handwriting analysis is not something that everyone can develop, and if it is going to work for you, it should work almost immediately. However, should this method of divination prove to be something with which you feel comfortable, experiment with it as much as possible. Only with time and much practice will the skill be perfected. Remember, it is better if the writer's gender and age are unknown to you, because these things should become apparent once you have mastered this particular skill.

Psychic handwriting analysis is not the same as the method used by some clairvoyants to give what they call 'postal readings'. Although the process appears to be the same, the whole concept of psychic handwriting analysis is different, inasmuch as the information and the way it is gleaned from the writing is processed by the image-making faculty of the brain, and not just through the practitioner's skill of clairvoyance or mediumship. Although it sounds very technical, the process of psychic handwriting analysis is quite simple. Should you have an aptitude for this method of divination it will just happen without any great effort.

In my case I find that simply by glancing briefly at someone's handwriting, images and pictures flash almost immediately through my mind. Sometimes just by glancing at a sample of writing, fragrances and physical sensations overwhelm me. When psychic handwriting analysis initially began to develop for me, I found it difficult to interpret what I was experiencing. It was only with time that I discovered that I had to allow my imagination to process the information, without any interpretation on my part.

Living with Psychic Ability

Once your psychic abilities have been fully established, and you have learned to use them with some degree of confidence and accuracy, you may occasionally be overwhelmed with the feeling that you can almost control circumstances, and that you can predict anything at any time. In the initial stages of your development it is quite common to feel as though your psychic skills are so acutely sharp that nothing or no one can faze you. You can rest assured that you will not always feel like this – and a good job too!

Do not allow yourself to become too complacent about your newly developed abilities. Although you may have worked hard at developing and refining your psychic skills, they will always need to be maintained. Just like the muscles of the physical body, if they are not exercised occasionally they will atrophy in time. It is simply not true that you can never lose your psychic skills once they have been developed. The instinctive faculties our prehistoric forebears relied on for their survival are simply not required by modern man, and so they have been completely lost. Although we still possess them potentially, their development is solely dependent upon use.

As a young boy I used to exercise my skills by using a simple guessing game, designed to keep my abilities active. Although I did this primarily to pass the time away, I now know that it was a mental exercise to help me.

Try this: sitting by a window in a front room of your home try to predict how many cars are going to pass by in a period of five minutes. Then extend this to ten minutes, and so on. This may seem like a childish exercise, but when you have successfully predicted the correct number of cars over a period of one hour, you should then see that the exercise is anything other than 'guesswork', particularly when you also predict the colour of the car, and even the make and model.

Try to predict the number of birds that will fly onto the roof of the house opposite, or even which bird will be the first to fly away. With this guessing exercise you should be looking to achieve a success rate of 20 out of 20 or more, rather than 5 out of 20. The more you practise the more accurate your predictions will be, dismissing any suggestions of the law of probability and chance.

Also as a child I would see faces in the patterns on curtains or the carpet. This is sometimes an indication that the clairvoyant skill is developing and is a phenomenon quite common with psychic children. Occasionally I would see faces in the clouds, and would attempt to move the clouds using the power of my mind.

Sometimes this would work with astonishing results. The point I am making is that to encourage the precipitation of the creative and psychic skills you should exercise your mind as much as possible. Rather than just sit lazily daydreaming, exercise the mental processes and allow your imagination some freedom.

The Final Word

My holistic approach to psychic development is intended for the cultivation of extended awareness on all levels of consciousness. It matters not whether you are an aspiring psychic or medium, or simply seeking to take greater control of your life, the methods given in this book should help you reach your goal. Just as the power and strength of the physical body can be improved with rigorous exercise and training, so too can the mind be exercised to increase its performance and efficiency. Although I have taken every measure to ensure that you enjoy using the exercises and techniques in this book, if they are to work you will need to apply yourself with consistency, discipline and determination.

Although the whole process of psychic development is exciting, it should in no way be taken too lightly. During the cultivation of the faculties, changes occur in the brain and nerve centres, and these changes will at some point have a psychological and emotional effect on you, at least until your nervous system becomes accustomed to the changes imposed upon it.

Although today there is a great deal of interest in the paranormal and psychic science, the subject has also rekindled an interest in the 100-year-old pseudoscience termed 'parapsychology', devoted primarily to the study of paranormal phenomena, such as telepathy, telekinesis, clairvoyance, mediumship and so on. Parapsychologists' studies of the paranormal are designed primarily to discredit the abilities of psychics and mediums and not really to support them, dismissing the information given by psychics as being no more than 'cold reading'; generalized data that could apply to anyone. Psychologist Paul Meehl described so-called 'cold reading' as The Barnum Effect, which he named after the famous circus owner, Phineas Taylor Barnum, a master psychological manipulator, who was known for his claim, 'We have something for everybody'. The Forer Effect, named after psychologist Bertram Forer, asserts that people who consult clairvoyants, etc. tend to accept vague and ambiguous statements as being personal to them, without realizing that the information they are accepting could really apply to anyone. Parapsychologists appear to have a rational explanation for all alleged paranormal phenomena, attributing them all to either psychological or natural occurrences, or even chance and probability.

Apophenia is the name that was coined by Klaus Conrad to describe the psychological phenomenon of 'seeing patterns or connections in random or meaningless data'. *Pareidolia* is a similar psychological phenomenon involving the discovery of sounds or images in random stimuli. For example, when taking a shower the running water might give you the impression that someone is calling your name, or that a phone is ringing when it is not.

When involved in the Victorian pastime of so-called 'table-tipping', don't be too pleased with the results when the table begins to move, or when the pointer shoots quickly across the Ouija board. The parapsychologists' explanation for this phenomenon is *ideomotor action*; body movements affected more by thought rather than by external stimuli.

The reason I have mentioned these things at the end of the book is to stipulate the importance of knowledge to support your newly developed abilities. Today it is not simply enough to possess psychic skills alone when standing up to the critical attacks from parapsychologists and sceptics; you need to also possess the answers and be able to come back with a quick and intelligent retort. Arm yourself with an extensive knowledge of the subject for which you have appointed yourself ambassador, and when confronted by parapsychologists and other sceptical academics, adopt the attitude, 'Attack is the best form of defence'.

Remember the ancient precept: 'The Thousand-Mile Journey Begins With a Single Step'. Now that you have read this book and mastered the techniques in its pages, you have taken that first step.

Index